FURNITURE
ROJECTS
r the DECK
nd LAWN

FURNITURE PROJECTS
for the DECK *and* LAWN

ATTRACTIVE 2x4 WOODWORKING

PROJECTS <u>ANYONE</u> CAN BUILD

TEXT, DRAWINGS, & PHOTOS BY John Kelsey

PROJECT DESIGN BY Ian J. Kirby

CAMBIUM PRESS

Bethel

FURNITURE PROJECTS FOR THE DECK AND LAWN

ISBN 1-892836-17-3
First printing: June 2004
Printed in the United States of America

Published by
    Cambium Press
    PO Box 909
    57 Stony Hill Road
    Bethel, CT 06801
            tel 203-778-2782   email cambiumpress@aol.com

Library of Congress Cataloging-in-Publication Data

Kelsey, John, 1946-
  Furniture projects for the deck and lawn : attractive 2x4 woodworking projects
anyone can build / text, drawings, and photos by John Kelsey ; project design and
construction by Ian J. Kirby.
      p. cm.
  Includes bibliographical references and index,
  1. Outdoor furniture. 2. Furniture making. I. Kirby, Ian J., 1932- II. Title.

TT197.5.09K47 2004
684.1'8--dc22

                                                        2004010183

CONTENTS

DECK CHAIR

Forget those metal rust traps, make these nifty wooden chairs instead

Every deck needs chairs, but most people make do with aluminum folders or plastic-coated steel ones from the home center. They sag or rust and chip, so every few years you have to buy some more. But it doesn't have to be that way, because here is a deck chair you can build yourself. It's a simple construction that relies on standard 1× and 2× lumber. The only tricky maneuver is cross-cutting some of the parts at a 10-degree angle, which you can do with any kind of saw and a home-made crosscut jig.

The chair is sized for a standard cushion, though you don't actually need any cushion because the wooden slats have just enough give to cradle your old bones comfortably.

The chair goes together quickly. It would only be a weekend project to make a suite of six of them. However, if you do decide to make a lot of chairs, start by completing one. This is because the exact length of the seat spacer depends on the precise width of your lumber. Once you go through it once, you'll be able to cut a stack of spacers at the same setting.

The roundover profile on the edges of the back slats and seat slats is an optional detail. It does make the chair a little more comfortable, but if you don't have an electric router, you can get equivalent results by sanding the slats. Use 80-grit paper wrapped around a scrap of wood, as shown in the photo on page 9.

DECK CHAIR

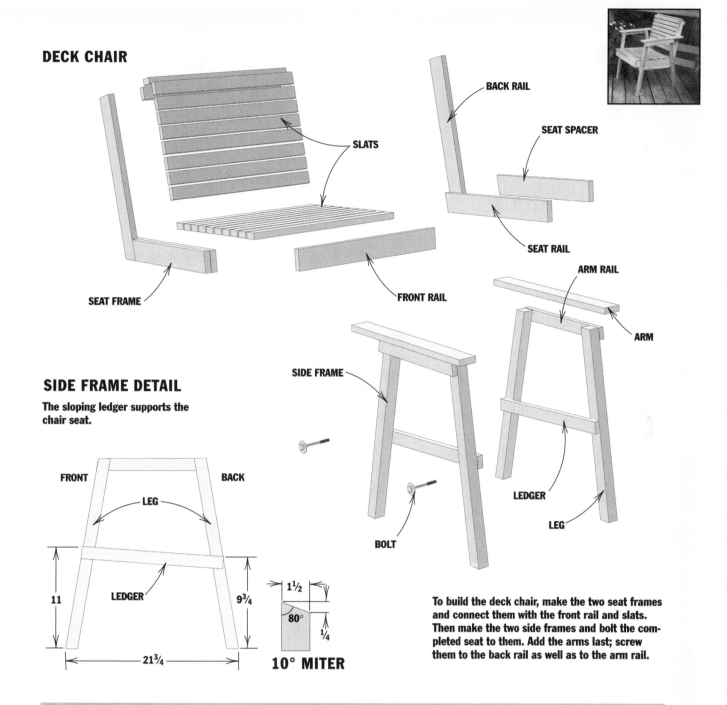

SLATS

BACK RAIL

SEAT SPACER

SEAT RAIL

ARM RAIL

ARM

SEAT FRAME

FRONT RAIL

SIDE FRAME

LEDGER

LEG

BOLT

SIDE FRAME DETAIL

The sloping ledger supports the chair seat.

FRONT   **BACK**

LEG

LEDGER

11

9¾

21¾

1½

80°

¼

10° MITER

To build the deck chair, make the two seat frames and connect them with the front rail and slats. Then make the two side frames and bolt the completed seat to them. Add the arms last; screw them to the back rail as well as to the arm rail.

YOUR INVESTMENT

Time: One day
Money: $33

SHOPPING LIST

8 feet 2×2 pine
48 feet 1×2 pine
16 feet of 1×3 pine
Four ¼ x 3½-inch galvanized hex-head machine bolts with nuts and washers
#6 × 2-inch galvanized screws
#6 × 1¼-inch galvanized screws
2-inch galvanized siding nails
2½-inch galvanized siding nails

PROJECT SPECS

The chair measures 30 inches high,
27 inches wide, and 22 inches front to back.

CUTTING LIST

PART	QTY.	DIMENSIONS	NOTES
Seat rail	2	¾ × 2½ × 20	1×3; miter one end 10°
Back rail	2	¾ × 2½ × 20	1×3; miter one end 10°
Seat spacer	2	¾ × 2½ × 17½	1×3; miter one end 10°
Front rail	1	¾ × 2½ × 20	1×3
Slat	20	¾ × 1½ × 20	1×2
Leg	4	1½ × 1½ × 24	2×2; miter both ends 10°
Arm rail	2	¾ × 1½ × 14¼	1×2; miter both ends 10°
Seat ledger	2	¾ × 1½ × 18	1×2
Arm	2	¾ × 1½ × 21	1×3

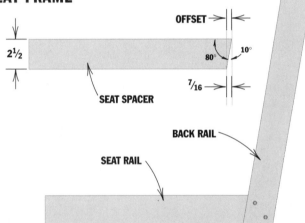

Join the first seat rail and back rail. Overlap the angled ends of the wood, use your square to make them flush, and draw a layout line (above). Glue and screw the rails together. Don't put a screw in the center of the joint because a bolt goes there (right).

DETAIL OF SEAT FRAME

To lay out a 10° miter on 2½-inch wide wood, measure an offset of ⁷/₁₆ inch and connect that point to the opposite corner. On 1½-inch wood, the offset is ¼ inch.

OFFSET

2½

80°   10°

⁷/₁₆

SEAT SPACER

BACK RAIL

SEAT RAIL

Join the other seat rail and back rail. Set the second set of parts on top of the first and draw layout lines before drilling, gluing and screwing the parts together. The two seat frames are mirror images of one another.

BUILDING THE DECK CHAIR

1 Saw the wood. Cut all the parts to the lengths given in the cutting list. The seat rails, back rails, front rail and arms are all the same size, ¾ inch by 2½ inches by 20 inches, so saw a total of seven pieces to that dimension. The seat rails, back rails, and seat spacers have to be mitered 10 degrees, or sawn at an angle of 10 degrees off square, on one end; the four legs are sawn to the same 10-degree angle on both ends. Note that the leg miters must be parallel to one another.

2 Join the first seat rail and back rail. The seat rail and the back rail make an L-shaped frame that is splayed open by the miters sawn on the ends of the wood. This angle is what makes the seat comfortable. However, there's a right seat frame and a left frame, so make one of them and then use it as a guide for making the other, in Step 3. Overlap the angled ends of the two pieces of wood and draw a layout line where they will be joined together, as shown in the photo above left. Drill pilot holes for two screws, avoiding the center of the overlap because a bolt goes there later on. Spread glue, align the parts with care, and drive the two screws home.

3 Join the other seat rail and back rail. The second seat rail and back rail connect exactly the same way as the pair you just joined, except for their handedness. To work out the right frame and the left frame, set the parts up with spacer

blocks, as shown in the photograph below left. Draw the layout lines, drill the pilot holes and spread the glue as in the previous step, but drive only one of the two screws. Then put the two seat frames together and adjust the parts until the angles are the same. Then drive the second screw.

4 Add the seat spacers. The seat spacers butt against the back rails and are flush with the seat rails. Their purpose is to make the outside of the seat and back assembly into a flat plane, to which you can attach the chair's arms and legs. Since 1× pine varies somewhat in width, the length of the seat spacer has to be trimmed to fit. Set the spacer in place with its mitered end against the back rail. Its other end should come flush with the front of the seat rail. Mark the length, saw off the excess wood, then glue and screw the seat spacer to the seat rail, as shown in the photo above right. Drill pilot holes for the four 1¼-inch screws.

5 Profile the slats. The 1×2 slats connect the two sides of the chair, and form the sitting surfaces. This is a simple chair without body-shaped curves, but you can improve its friendliness by rounding the sharp corners off the slats. Use a ¼-inch roundover cutter in an electric router, as shown in the photo above right. If you don't have a router, you can achieve equivalent results by sanding. with 80-grit paper wrapped around a block of wood. You don't have to remove much material to soften up the way the chair sits.

Add the seat spacers. Glue and screw the seat spacers to the seat rail.

Profile the slats. Use an electric router with a ¼-inch roundover cutter to remove the sharp edges of the slats (above). Instead of routing, you can sand the sharp corners off the wood (right).

6 Attach the front rail. The front rail connects the two seat frames. It establishes the width of the seat, stiffens the construction, and covers the end grain of the seat rails. Glue it, and nail it in place with the 2½-inch siding nails. Be sure to spread glue on the ends of the seat rails and seat spacers as well as on the face of the front rail. Start two nails near each end of the front rail, then stand the seat frame up on end as shown at right, so you can drive the nails home. Set the seat down on the worktable to make sure it's still flat, then stand it on end again to drive two more nails into each joint.

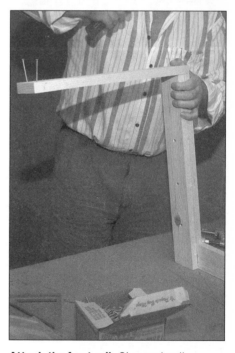

Attach the front rail. Glue and nail the front rail to the seat rail and seat spacer. Stand the seat frame on end to drive the nails home.

Space and nail the seat slats. Spread glue along the front rail and nail the slat in place with 2-inch siding nails. The narrow stick at the bottom left is the spacing gauge (above). Using the spacing gauge to locate the slats, glue and nail seat slats until you reach the back uprights (below).

Square the seat. Clamp the seat to the worktable and use a seat slat to gauge its width at the back, then measure the diagonals. Push the construction until the diagonals are equal.

7 Square the seat. The next step is to nail the slats to the front rails, but first make sure the construction is square. Clamp the seat frame to the worktable. Since the slats are the same length as the front rail, use one of them to gauge the width at the back of the seat. To verify that it is square, measure the diagonals as shown in the photo above. If they are not equal, loosen one clamp and push the diagonals equal. Then clamp the seat down tight.

8 Space and nail the seat slats. The seat slats and the back slats are exactly the same. Glue and nail the first slat to the front of the seat. Spread the glue right across the top of the front rail. Attach the slat with 2-inch siding nails. The remainder of the slats should be spaced ¼ inch apart. Find or make a wooden gauge of this thickness and use it to locate the next slat, as shown in the photos above right. Dab some glue on the underside of the slat and attach it to the seat rails with two nails at each end. Continue to add slats until you reach the back.

9 Slat the back. Unclamp the construction and flip it over so you can continue gluing and nailing slats to the back rails. Start at the top of the back and work

Slat the back. Flip the construction so the back is on the worktable, and continue gluing and nailing the slats in place. Start at the top and work toward the seat.

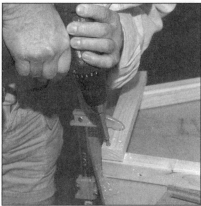

Complete the back. Nail and glue a slat on top of the back rails and another on the back-side of the chair.

Join one arm rail to two legs.
Align the arm rail at the top of the legs, with the angled cuts flush at the edges of the parts. Glue and screw the arm to one leg (left). Measure the outside width at the open side of the U shape. Adjust the width to 21¾ inches, then attach the arm rail to the other leg (below).

toward the seat, spacing the slats with the ¼-inch gauge. However, don't fill in the entire back. For comfort, stop two slats, or about four inches, from the seat and leave the back open at this point.

10 Complete the back. To complete the back, glue and nail a slat on top of the back rails and another on the back side of the chair, as shown in the photo above. Now you're ready to move on to the structure of the chair legs and arms.

11 Join one arm rail to two legs. One arm rail and two legs make a U-shaped unit, which forms the side frame of the chair. Start by aligning the arm rail at the top of one of the legs so the angled cuts come flush with the edges of the parts. Draw a layout line, spread glue, clamp the parts together, drill pilot holes for a pair of 2-inch screws, and drive the screws. Now spread glue and clamp the other leg in position and measure the outside width at the open end of the U shape. Adjust the width to 21¾ inches before you screw the parts together, as shown in the photo at top right.

Add the seat ledger. Draw layout lines to locate the seat ledger on the legs, then glue and screw it in place. It goes on the opposite side from the arm rail.

12 Add the seat ledger. The seat ledger completes the side frame. It will support the seat assembly. The seat ledger slopes with respect to the floor.

Measure up from the bottom of the legs as shown on the drawing on page 7 to locate the seat ledger. Be sure the seat ledger goes on the opposite side

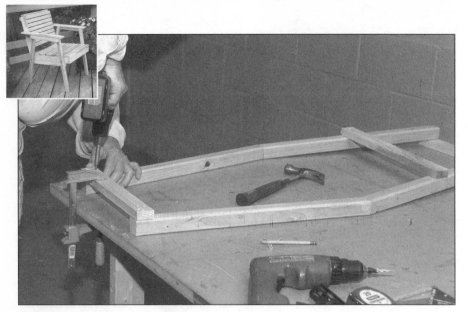

of the leg from the arm rail. Draw layout lines, then glue and screw the parts together with 2-inch screws through the ledger into the chair legs. This completes one side frame.

13 **Make the second side frame.** The second side frame should be exactly the same as the one you just completed, except one is right-handed and the other is left-handed. Begin by joining the arm rail to the two legs as you did in Step 11. Instead of measuring the width between the legs, use the completed side frame as a gauge, as shown in the photo at top left. Up to this point the two frames are the same. Now clamp the two frames together in the orientation they'll have in the completed chair, as shown in the photo below left, with the arm rails to the outside of the sandwich and the seat ledger trapped between the chair legs. This allows you to transfer the location of the seat ledger from one side frame to the other. Take the sandwich apart and complete the second side frame.

Make the second side frame. Glue and screw the remaining arm to the other two legs. Use the completed side frame to gauge the width (above). Clamp both side frames together, with the ledger in the middle. Transfer the location of the seat ledger from one frame to the other (below).

14 **Join the seat to the side frames.** The chair seat rests on the ledgers. It's held by two bolts in holes drilled through the legs and seat rails. Set the seat assembly on its side on the worktable and position the first side frame on it, as shown in the photo at right. The seat ledger fits tightly underneath the seat spacer, with its high end to the front of the chair. If everything looks right except the low end of the ledger is at the front, you've got the wrong side frame. Get the other one, or else turn the

Attach the arms. Clamp the arms to the arm rails and drive screws from the inside of the back rails.

Join the seat to the side frames. Set the seat assembly on its side and position a side frame on it. The seat ledger fits tightly under the seat spacer, with its high end toward the front. Align the low end of the ledger with the bottom corner of the back rail. Glue and bolt the parts together.

chair seat over. Align the low end of the seat ledger with the bottom of the back rail. Clamp the parts in position and drill a ¼-inch bolt hole through each leg, down through the back rail or seat spacer and seat rail. Unclamp the assembly so you can spread glue, then insert the bolts. The bolt head goes to the outside, with the nut under the chair seat. Put a washer under the bolt head and another washer under the nut. Tighten the bolt so the washers bite into the wood, as shown in the photo above. Turn the assembly over to bolt the other side frame to the chair seat.

15 Make the arms. The chair arms complete the structure of the chair, by tying the side frames into the back rails. A square connection at the back rail is important, but the rest of

the arm should be smooth and friendly to the touch. Draw a line 4 inches from one end of each arm, and round over all the corners and edges except for the two long edges within the 4-inch marks.

16 Attach the arms. Plant the arms on the arm rails so they are flush with the rear of the back rails. Mark where the arms cross the back rails, then remove them to drill pilot holes for two screws through each back rail. Spread glue where the parts cross one another. Clamp the arms to the arm rails, and drive 2½-inch screws through from inside the back, as shown in the photo at top right. Nail the arms to the arm rails with 2-inch siding nails.

17 Finish the chair. Go over the chair with the ¼-inch roundover

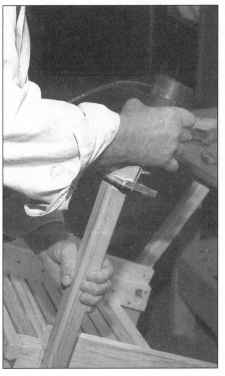

Finish the chair. Rout the corners off the bottom of the legs so they won't splinter when being dragged.

cutter in the router. Remove any sharp edge you think might cause discomfort. Also rout the corners off the bottom of the legs. This will make the chair easy to drag across your deck or patio. Paint the chair, or varnish it, or leave it unfinished to weather naturally.

LAWN TABLE

Handy enough for dinner or drinks, it's nice enough to take inside

When you entertain out-doors, you need little tables for drinks, snacks and buffet meals. This little table is good-looking, sturdy and versatile. It's attractive enough to come indoors for the winter.

The table has been designed to fit alongside a chair, or in front of it. It's light and easy to move. There are no tricky cuts

or difficult gluing maneuvers, so it's quick to make. You can make two or three in hardly more time than the first one takes.

If you do get into making multiple tables, you'll be able to tighten up on the shopping list. The table looks best when it's made of clear wood, so the shopping list has been inflated by a full 20%, to allow you to

work around knots. If you can find clear wood, you can reduce the quantities accordingly.

The shelf is a nice detail and it does help the table structurally, but it would be strong enough without it, so you can leave it off if you like. In that case, put the lower four leg blocks at the very bottom of the legs. They'll look better.

LAWN TABLE

Join pairs of leg pieces with blocks, add the caps, then connect the leg assemblies with the short and long rails. Make the shelf, then nail the table top to the rails.

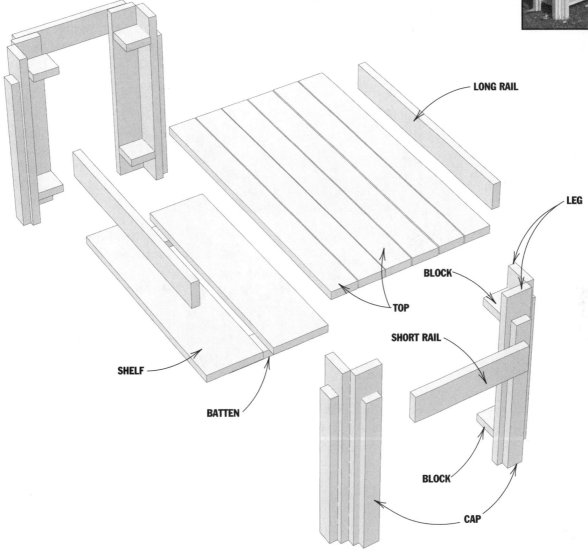

LONG RAIL

LEG

BLOCK

SHORT RAIL

BLOCK

CAP

TOP

SHELF

BATTEN

YOUR INVESTMENT
__Time: One evening__
__Money: $18__

SHOPPING LIST
12 feet 1×2 pine
40 feet 1×3 pine
6 feet 1×6 pine
#6 × 1¼-inch galvanized screws
2-inch galvanized siding nails

PROJECT SPECS
The lawn table is 26 inches long, 16 inches wide, and 18¼ inches high.

CUTTING LIST

PART	QTY.	DIMENSIONS	NOTES
Leg	8	¾ × 2½ × 17½	1×3
Cap	8	¾ × 1½ × 15	1×2
Block	8	¾ × 2½ × 2½	1×3
Short rail	2	¾ × 2½ × 11	1×3
Long rail	2	¾ × 2½ × 21	1×3
Shelf	2	¾ × 5½ × 22	1×6
Batten	2	¾ × 2½ × 7	1×3
Top	6	¾ × 2 ½ × 26	1×3

BUILDING THE TABLE

1 Cut all the wood. All the saw cuts are made at right angles, but two of the lengths are critical. They are the lengths of the eight cap pieces and of the twelve little blocks, which both depend on the width of your 1×3 pine. The length of the cap, plus the width of the 1×3 rails, has to equal the length of the leg. The length of the block equals the width of the 1×3.

2 Block the legs. Two leg pieces joined corner to corner make up each right-angle leg. They're held together by a pair of blocks inside each leg. Begin by gluing and screwing two blocks to the inside face of four of the leg pieces. In the next step, you'll add the other leg piece. The blocks fit their own length in from either end of the leg pieces. Roll glue on the edge of a block, position it as shown in the photo at left, and drill a clearance hole through the face of the leg. Then drive a single 2-inch screw through the leg and into the block. Join the other blocks and legs in the same way.

3 Add the second leg pieces. To complete a right-angle leg, roll glue onto the edge of both blocks and position the second leg piece. Drill a clearance hole through the face of the leg piece into each block and drive the 2-inch screws, as shown in the photo at below. Complete the other three legs in the same way.

Block the legs. Gauge the block placement with another block. Glue and screw two blocks to each of four leg pieces.

Add the second leg pieces. Roll glue onto the edge of the blocks, but not on the leg piece. (above). Screw the second leg piece to the blocks (right).

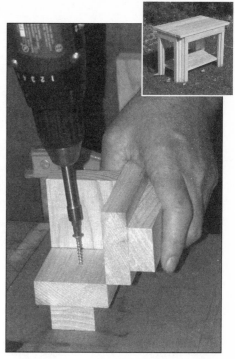

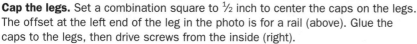

Cap the legs. Set a combination square to ½ inch to center the caps on the legs. The offset at the left end of the leg in the photo is for a rail (above). Glue the caps to the legs, then drive screws from the inside (right).

4 Cap the legs. The caps fit on the outside of the leg pieces. They support the rails, and cover the screw heads. The caps fit flush with one end of the legs, leaving space for the rails at the other end. The caps are an inch narrower than the legs, so you can center them with a combination square set to ½ inch, as shown in the photo above. Roll glue on the face of the cap, position it on the leg, and clamp it in place. Then fasten it with three of the 1¼-inch screws, driven from inside the leg. Because of the clamp, you can get away without clearance holes. Cap both faces of all four leg assemblies in the same way.

Join the short rails. Glue and clamp a short rail to the leg and screw the parts together (above). Add the second leg to the free end of the rail and tap the parts into line (right).

5 Join the short rails. The short rails connect the leg assemblies in pairs, forming the ends of the table. The short rails fit tight on top of the caps, aligned with the caps' outside edges. Hold the first short rail and leg together and draw a layout line. Spread glue, then clamp the short rail in place, as shown

in the photo above. Drill clearance holes to prevent the wood from splitting, and drive three of the 1¼-inch screws into the short rail through the back of the leg. Join the second leg assembly to the other end of the short rail. Make the other end of the table in the same way.

Join the end assemblies. Glue, clamp and screw the long rails between the end assemblies.

Make the shelf. Use blocks of scrap to center the battens on the shelf boards, and to maintain a uniform space between them.

6 Join the end assemblies. Now you have two table ends. Complete the table base by connecting the ends with the long rails. Screw the long rails to the legs in the same way as you joined the short rails in the previous step, as shown in the photo above.

7 Make the shelf. Make and install the shelf before you make the table top. The two battens connect the two shelf boards. Use scraps of wood to position the battens on the underside of the shelf, as shown in the photo at top right. A ¾-inch space separates the two shelf boards, with the battens centered from side to side and inset ¾ inch at the ends. Fasten the battens to the top boards with 1¼-inch screws.

8 Install the shelf. Drop the shelf onto the bottom blocks inside the legs. Clamp the shelf to the blocks and drive a 1¼-inch screw through each block into the shelf.

9 Center the table top. The six top boards overhang the base by ¼ inch all around. Mark the center of the short rails, and

Complete the table top. Then attach the edge boards, and fill in the spaces in between.

begin installing the top at the center. Place a board on either side of the center marks, with a gap of about ⅛ inch. Set a combination square to ¼ inch to equalize the overhang at either end. Attach the two center boards with two 2½-inch siding nails at each end.

10 Complete the table top. Use the combination square to align the outer boards of the top with the table base, nail them in

place, and fill in the remaining space. Space the siding nails with care, so their heads make a regular pattern.

11 Prepare the table for finishing. Wrap 100-grit sandpaper around a block of wood and knock the sharp corners off the table. Go over all of its edges, but don't sand so much that you destroy the crispness of the design. Sanding brings any inaccuracies into line.

TABLE STAKE

Quick project uses up scrap, dresses up garden parties

You're planning a garden party and how can people have a good time when they must juggle drinks along with plates of chicken wings?

These little stake tables can do the trick.

Each stake makes a little table at whatever height you want. They're made entirely out of scrap, so they couldn't be simpler or quicker to make. You can keep them for next time, or toss them away and make more.

The basic stake is a pine 1x2, anywhere between 18 and 30 inches long. The shelf is any square piece of scrap wood. It's glued and screwed or nailed to the stake. You can leave the shelves square, or else jigsaw them into circles or ovals.

MAKING THE STAKES

1 Gather the scrap wood. You'll probably have to saw some of it out of larger offcuts. Saw squares for the shelves.

2 Sharpen the stakes. Use the jigsaw to whittle a point on the stakes. Draw the point freehand, about a hand-span long. Saw the two sides of the stake, then saw one face of it.

3 Make the shelf. Square a line across the face of the stake, a couple of inches down from the top end. Drill two clearance holes through the stake. Smear some glue on it. Drive the screws through the stake into the edge of the shelf, pulling it tight.

4 Install the furniture. Once you decide where to plant the stake, tap it about six inches into the ground with your hammer.

Sharpen the stakes. Draw a layout line and jigsaw the point on the stakes. Saw toward the point

Make the shelf. Glue and screw the stake to the edge of the shelf.

DRINK STAKE

Sharpen the stake, then attach the shelf to it.

SHELF

STAKE

CUTTING LIST

PART	QTY.	DIMENSION	NOTES
Stake	1	$\frac{3}{4} \times 1\frac{1}{2} \times 28$	From scrap
Shelf	1	$\frac{3}{4} \times 5\frac{1}{2} \times 5\frac{1}{2}$	From scrap

YOUR INVESTMENT

Time: 10 minutes
Money: 10 cents

SHOPPING LIST

#6 × 2-inch galvanized screws

ADIRONDACK CHAIR

Here's a summer delight
you can build in a long evening

The Adirondack chair is a great example of carpenter ingenuity. It's surprisingly comfortable, and perfect for sitting out on a summer evening. You can kick back, sip a long drink, and forget all about the high price of car repairs or whatever else might ail you.

The level arm with the angled seat and back make the Adirondack chair look complicated to build, but it is not. The important angles come from direct linear measurement, with no need for protractors or bevel gauges. The seat rail and the back leg are the same sloping piece of wood. The whole thing comes out of standard lumber with a few easy angle cuts. Just follow the dimensions given in the drawings, and your chair will come out right.

While it's possible to set up the angled cuts on the chop saw, it's easier, quicker and safer to handsaw them, as shown in the steps that follow. However, you do need to have a sharp saw—your old tree-pruning saw won't do the job. If you shop for a hand saw, look for a short blade with long, shark-style teeth. Stanley and Sandvik both make short toolbox saws that are exactly right for this kind of work.

In the Adirondacks, they make these chairs out of white

An Adirondack ottoman (page 28) completes your outdoor living room.

Join the front legs. Roll glue on the front leg brace, and nail the front leg to it. Make sure the ends and edges are flush.

cedar. Down here on the flat land cedar can be somewhat expensive, so we use regular lumberyard 1× pine, which we paint. For a rich alternative, make the chair in redwood. Then decide whether to varnish it, which means renewing the varnish annually, or to leave it unfinished.

Plane or sand the sharp edges and corners off all the pieces of wood, either before you start assembling the chair or as you go along. This makes the chair more comfortable, and it also makes it easier to paint.

BUILDING THE CHAIR

1 Crosscut all the wood. All the parts come from standard widths of 1× lumberyard pine, which is ¾ inch thick. Crosscut all the parts to the finished lengths given on the next page before you fit anything together. Cut two extra pieces of scrap to the same length as the front legs, 20 inches. You'll use them as props in Step 12.

2 Join the front legs. Glue and nail the front leg braceto the front leg, to make a composite leg that is L-shaped in cross section. Roll glue onto the edge of the brace. Set the front leg in position on it, making sure the edges and ends are flush. Nail

ADIRONDACK CHAIR

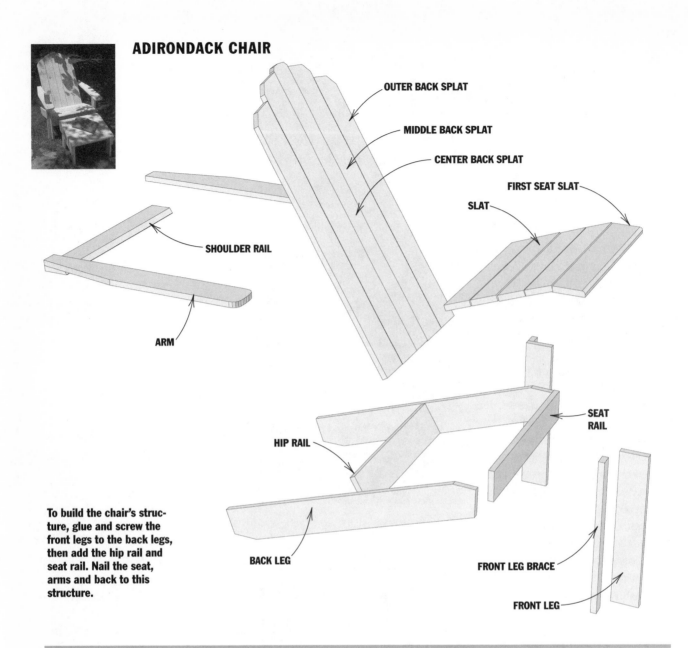

OUTER BACK SPLAT

MIDDLE BACK SPLAT

CENTER BACK SPLAT

FIRST SEAT SLAT

SLAT

SHOULDER RAIL

ARM

HIP RAIL

SEAT RAIL

BACK LEG

FRONT LEG BRACE

FRONT LEG

To build the chair's structure, glue and screw the front legs to the back legs, then add the hip rail and seat rail. Nail the seat, arms and back to this structure.

YOUR INVESTMENT
Time: One day
Money: $35

SHOPPING LIST
4 feet 1×2 pine
20 feet 1×4 pine
36 feet 1×5 pine
3-inch galvanized spiral deck nails
2-inch galvanized spiral deck nails
#6 × 2-inch galvanized screws
#6 × 1¼-inch galvanized screws

PROJECT SPECS
The chair is 38 inches high, 37 inches front to back, and 31 inches wide at the arms.

CUTTING LIST

PART	QTY.	DIMENSIONS	NOTES
Front leg	2	¾ × 3½ × 20	
Front leg brace	2	¾ × 1½ × 20	
Back leg	2	¾ × 4½ × 37	
Hip rail	1	¾ × 4½ × 22	
Seat slat	4	¾ × 3½ × 23¾	
Seat rail	1	¾ × 4 × 23½	Round one edge
First seat slat	1	¾ × 4 × 23½	Optional bevel on one edge
Arm	2	¾ × 4½ × 31	
Shoulder rail	1	¾ × 3½ × 26¼	Optional bevel on one edge
Outside back splat	2	¾ × 4½ × 36½	
Middle back splat	2	¾ × 4½ × 39¼	
Center back splat	1	¾ × 3½ × 40	

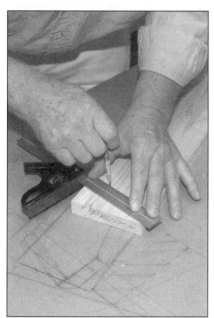

BACK LEG LAYOUT

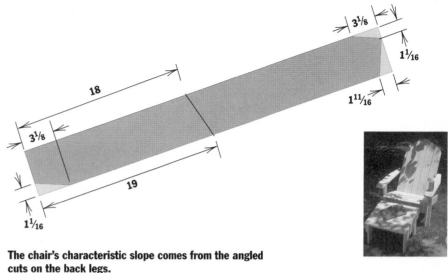

$3\frac{1}{8}$

$1\frac{1}{16}$

18

$1\frac{11}{16}$

$3\frac{1}{8}$

19

$1\frac{1}{16}$

The chair's characteristic slope comes from the angled cuts on the back legs.

Lay out the back legs. Draw the angled cuts from the measurements given in the drawing. It may help you to make a full-size layout of the chair side, like the design drawing that's visible on the surface of the worktable.

each composite leg together with five 2-inch spiral deck nails.

3 Lay out the back legs. The two back legs are identical, so it's best to lay out both of them at the same time. Mark the front and back ends of the wood. Measure 19 inches from the back bottom corner and 18 inches from the back top corner. Connect these points and extend the lines all the way around the wood. These lines will locate the hip rail. Lay out the angled cuts at the back and front of the back legs, as shown in the drawing above. These cuts establish the slope of the back leg and seat.

4 Saw the back legs. Saw the angled cuts with a jigsaw or with a handsaw. With the jigsaw, be sure you are using a blade for cutting wood. With a sharp handsaw in soft pine, the weight of the saw does the work—all you do is steer. If you lean on

Saw the back legs. To make the angled cuts, clamp the wood to the worktable (above). Clamp both legs together in the vise to saw both at once (right).

the saw, you'll make a rough cut with a lot of splinters. Clamp the wood to the worktable, or grab it in a vise, so you can concentrate on sawing straight instead of on holding things still.

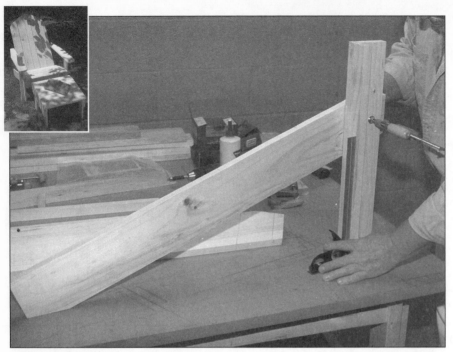

Join the back legs to the front legs. Clamp the front leg to the back leg. The top of the back leg should be 16 inches above the table, while the front leg should be square to the table and inset 1 inch from the end of the back leg (left). Glue and screw the front leg to the back leg (above).

Nail the hip rail. Use scrap blocks to clamp the hip rail to the back leg, in front of the layout lines drawn in Step 3. Nail from the outside of the back leg.

6 Nail the hip rail. The hip rail, which is 22 inches long, is the structural center of the chair. Its length establishes the chair's overall width as well as the size of the seat and back parts. Clamp a block of scrap to the back side of the layout line you drew in Step 3. Then clamp the hip rail to the block of scrap, as shown at left. Drive three 3-inch spiral nails through the face of the back leg, into the end of the hip rail. Clamp the other leg assembly to the other end of the hip rail, and drive three more nails.

7 Add the seat rail. The seat rail spans the front of the chair, underneath the front edge of the seat. It's nailed into the ends of the back legs with 3-inch spiral nails. These nails are close to the end of the rail, so drill pilot holes to prevent splitting. To keep the chair from skidding around while you nail, clamp a stop board to the worktable, as shown in the photo at the top of the next page.

5 Join the back legs to the front legs. Set the parts in position on the worktable, as shown in the top photo, with the top of the back leg 16 inches up the front leg assembly. The front leg fits an inch behind the front end of the back leg. Draw layout lines on both parts. Roll glue onto the faces of the back legs, inside these layout lines. Clamp the parts together, drill pilot holes and screw through the back leg into the front leg. Drive 2-inch screws into the front leg brace and 1¼-inch screws into the leg itself. Be sure you end up with a right side and a left side—the two should mirror one another.

8 **Shape the seat slats.** The first seat slat, which is level, has a rounded front edge so it doesn't cut into your legs. Shape it with a ⅜-inch round-over cutter in the router, or rasp it with a Surform. The next slat makes the transition from level to the slope beneath your thighs. As an option, you can bevel its front edge. This narrows the gap toward the first slat. You can saw the bevel at 20 degrees on the table saw, or you can rasp it to a line ¼-inch off one edge of the wood.

9 **Nail the seat.** The first seat slat sits flat on top of the seat rail, with its front edge overhanging by about ¹⁄₁₆ inch. Spread glue on the top edge of the seat rail. Nail the first seat slat to the back leg and to the seat rail, using the 2-inch spiral deck nails. Glue and nail the next slat with its beveled edge toward the front slat, leaving a small gap between the two slats. Now clamp a piece of scrap to the hip rail in the position the back splats will occupy, to act as a stop and to reserve the thickness of the splats. Fit a seat slat tight against the scrap and nail it in place. Arrange the remaining two seat slats in the space that's left, and nail them down.

10 **Shape the arms.** The arms have round ends and taper toward the back. Clamp the arms together face to face to lay out the taper shown in the drawing. Saw the taper with the jigsaw. Choose a suitable template to lay out the rounded end, such as a coffee can or a soda cup, as shown in the photo above right. Saw the curve with

Add the seat rail. The seat rail stabilizes the chair frame. The stop board at the far edge of the worktable keeps the assembly from skidding around while you drill pilot holes and nail the rail in place.

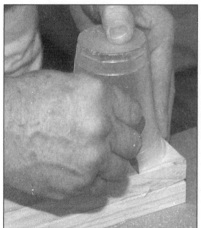

Shape the arms. Clamp the arms to the worktable and saw the taper with the jigsaw. The taper is 12 inches long and half as wide as the arm blank (left). Draw the arm radius around a suitable cup or can (right).

ARM LAYOUT

The shoulder rail supports the arm slats. Its beveled edge makes a neat fit with the back splats, but the bevel isn't structurally necessary.

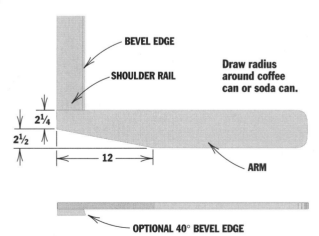

BEVEL EDGE

SHOULDER RAIL

Draw radius around coffee can or soda can.

2¼

2½

12

ARM

OPTIONAL 40° BEVEL EDGE

Connect the arms. Clamp the arms face down on the worktable, position the shoulder rail and screw the assembly together.

Fit the arms. Support the arm assembly with two 20-inch scrap props. To position the arms back to front, clamp back splats to the bottom rail and bring the shoulder rail up to them (above). When you like the position of the arms, drive 3-inch spiral nails down into the front legs (below).

the jigsaw, starting from the end and cutting toward the side. Sand or rasp the wood smooth.

11 Connect the arms. The shoulder rail connects the chair arms and supports the back splats. It will make a neat fit if you bevel one edge at 40 degrees, which you can lay out by measuring ½ inch from the corner of the wood. You can saw this bevel on the table saw, you can saw it with the jigsaw, you can plane it or you can omit it, because it is not structural. Clamp one arm face down on the worktable. Set the shoulder rail on it, with the bevel down and facing toward the front, as shown in the photo above left. Drive a 1¼-inch screw through the intersection, then square the pieces to one another. Drive three more screws. Repeat these steps to join the other arm to the shoulder rail, making a U-shape. The distance between the arms equals the hip rail, or 22 inches, and a bit wider is OK.

12 Fit the arms. Make two 20-inch props out of scrap to hold the chair arms in position while you nail them to the legs. Clamp the props to the back legs just behind the hip rail. Clamp two back splats to the hip rail. Set the arm subassembly in position and bring it forward until the two back splats rest against the edge of the shoulder rail. Center the arm assembly from side to side. When it looks exactly right, drive three 3-inch spiral nails down through the top of each arm and into the front legs.

13 Compose the back. You can make the back splats any shape you like. Lay the five boards together on the worktable. Draw the shape you want on the center board and the two boards on one side of it. Then clamp the boards together in matching pairs in order to cut the shapes with the jigsaw, the same way you made the arms.

14 Attach the back. Turn the chair upside down on the worktable. Slide one of the outside back splats into position. Spread glue and screw it to the hip rail, from underneath the seat. Use three 1¼-inch screws. Attach the other outside back splat in the same way. Next, draw a centerline on the shoulder rail in order to center the center splat. Finally, clamp the two middle splats in place and center them in their spaces. Screw them to the hip rail.

15 Anchor the back. You need some support before you can anchor the back splats, so reclamp the two props in position under the chair's arms. Drive two 3-inch spiral nails through each back leg into the edges of the outside back splats. Tuck a straightedge up under the chair arms and draw a layout line across the back. Drive two of the 2-inch spiral nails through each splat into the shoulder rail. Drive the nails ⅜ inch below the layout line, horizontal to the chair back. They should go straight into the edge of the shoulder rail. Now you can have a test sit.

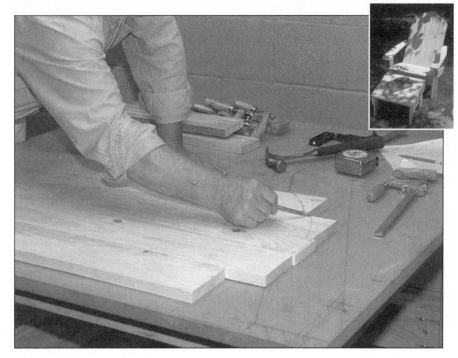

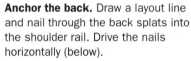

Compose the back. Lay the five back boards together on the worktable, and draw the back shape. It can be any shape you like.

Attach the back. Turn the chair upside down in order to attach the back splats. Glue and screw them to the inside face of the hip rail (left).

Anchor the back. Draw a layout line and nail through the back splats into the shoulder rail. Drive the nails horizontally (below).

ADIRONDACK OTTOMAN

The essential accessory for every mountain lodge

Every Adirondack chair needs a companion footstool. It transforms the rustic seat into a veritable Barcalounger. Just add a crystalline mountain lake plus a dollop of mosquito repellent, and you're on vacation.

BUILDING THE OTTOMAN

1 Cut the parts. The ottoman comes out of the same standard 1×4s and 1×5s as the Adiron-

Join the legs and rails. Glue and screw a long leg and a short leg to each long rail, making a pair of U-shapes.

dack chair on page 20. Crosscut all the parts to length.

2 Make the long rails. Lay out the 1×5 long rails, as shown in the drawing at right. Saw the angles with the handsaw, on the chopsaw or table saw, or with the jigsaw. The ottoman is rustic, and precision is not critical.

3 Join the legs and rails. Glue and screw a long leg and a short leg to each long rail, making a pair of U-shapes, one right-handed and the other left-handed. Use four of the 1¼-inch screws per intersection.

4 Join the hip rail. The hip rail connects the short legs. It fits against the inside edge of the short legs and butts against the long rails. Glue and nail the hip rail in place. Nail through the hip rail into the edge of the leg, and also nail through the long rail into the hip rail. Use 2-inch galvanized spiral nails.

5 Nail the first slat. The first slat rests on the long legs and on the flat at the top of the long rail, as shown in the drawing. Drive a pair of 3-inch spiral nails through the slat and into the end grain of each long leg.

6 Nail the front rail. Round-over the front edge of the front rail by sanding, rasping or routing. Nail the front rail onto the long legs of the ottoman with 2-inch spiral nails. The front rail should come up flush with the top surface of the first slat, and it should cover the ends of the long rails.

7 Nail the slats. Sand the sharp corners off the remaining slats and nail them to the long rails. Leave a gap of 1⁄16 inch to 1⁄8 inch from one slat to the next. Drive three 2-inch spiral nails through each end of each slat. Round-over the overhanging edge of the last slat.

8 Finish the ottoman. Paint the ottoman to match your Adirondack chair. Want two ottomen? It's quick and easy to make another. And another.

ADIRONDACK OTTOMAN

Glue and screw the legs to the long rail, add the hip rail and front rail, then nail the seat to this understructure.

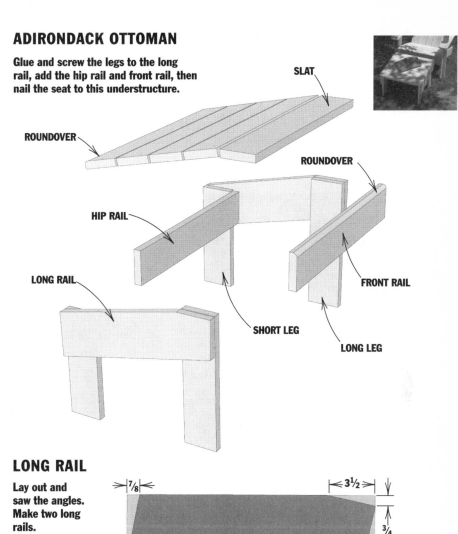

LONG RAIL

Lay out and saw the angles. Make two long rails.

7⁄8 3½ ¾ 7⁄8

YOUR INVESTMENT
<u>Time:</u> One evening
<u>Money:</u> $14

SHOPPING LIST
20 feet 1×4 pine
4 feet 1×5 pine
2-inch and 3-inch galvanized spiral deck nails
#6 × 1¼-inch galvanized screws

PROJECT SPECS
The ottoman is 15 inches high, 18 inches front to back and 21 inches wide.

CUTTING LIST

PART	QTY.	DIMENSIONS	NOTES
Long leg	2	¾ × 3½ × 13½	
Short leg	2	¾ × 3½ × 11	
Long rail	2	¾ × 4½ × 18	
Hip rail	1	¾ × 3½ × 19½	
Front rail	1	¾ × 3½ × 21	Round-over one edge
Slat	5	¾ × 3½ × 21	Sand sharp edges

PICNIC TABLE

A hearty board for the whole family, yet it wheels away
with the greatest of ease

Does anyone not have fond memories of whiling away summer afternoons around a picnic table in the park? With this kind of table you can carve your initials into the top and jump off the benches, spill cans of soda and chop garlic, and it all rolls right off. You can also spread a checkered cloth and have the whole family over for a barbecue, because a 6-foot-long table easily seats six people, or eight if some of them are children. And the table shown here can be built any length you like, up to 12 feet.

These days you can buy a picnic table at the home center. It'll probably cost you $200, and it won't be made with any care. If you make your own table you'll spend less than half the money, plus you'll be able to choose the wood and detail the table to suit yourself. You can work around big knots and pitch pockets, you can select top boards that more or less match, and you can avoid splintery

PICNIC TABLE

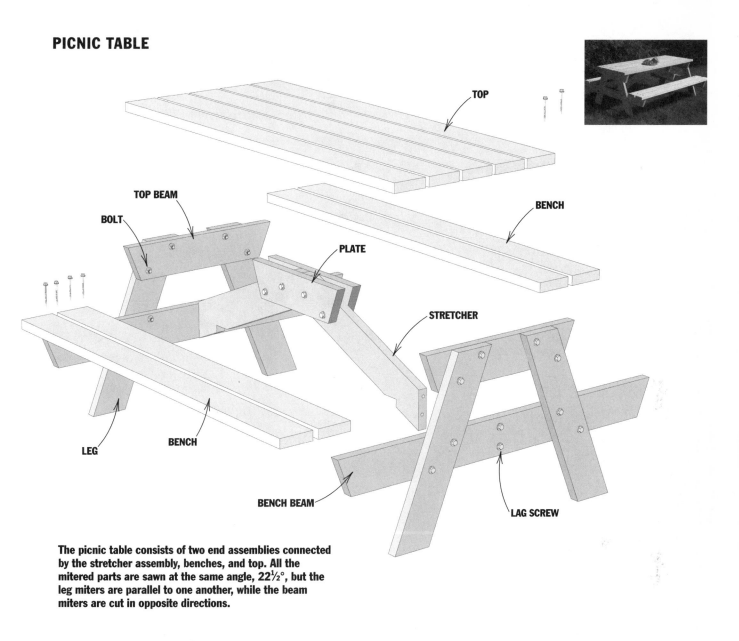

The picnic table consists of two end assemblies connected by the stretcher assembly, benches, and top. All the mitered parts are sawn at the same angle, 22½°, but the leg miters are parallel to one another, while the beam miters are cut in opposite directions.

YOUR INVESTMENT

Time: **One day**
Money: **$55 for wood, $35 for hardware**

PROJECT SPECS

The table with benches is 70 inches long, 60 inches wide and 29 inches high.

SHOPPING LIST

Eight 12-foot 2×6 planks
Sixteen $\frac{3}{8} \times 3\frac{1}{2}$-inch hex-head bolts with nuts and washers
Two $\frac{1}{2} \times 7$-inch hex-head bolts with nuts and washers
Four $\frac{3}{8} \times 5$-inch hex-head bolts with nuts and washers
Forty $\frac{1}{4} \times 3\frac{1}{2}$-inch lag screws with washers

CUTTING LIST

PART	QTY.	DIMENSIONS	NOTES
Bench	4	$1\frac{1}{2} \times 5\frac{5}{8} \times 70$	2×6
Top	5	$1\frac{1}{2} \times 5\frac{5}{8} \times 70$	2×6
Leg	4	$1\frac{1}{2} \times 5\frac{5}{8} \times 29$	2×6, miter both ends 22½°, parallel
Top beam	2	$1\frac{1}{2} \times 5\frac{5}{8} \times 28$	2×6, miter both ends 22½°, opposite
Bench beam	2	$1\frac{1}{2} \times 5\frac{5}{8} \times 59$	2×6, miter both ends 22½°, opposite
Stretcher	2	$1\frac{1}{2} \times 5\frac{5}{8} \times 33\frac{3}{8}$	2×6, miter both ends 22½°, parallel
Plate	2	$1\frac{1}{2} \times 5\frac{5}{8} \times 22$	2×6, miter both ends 22½°, opposite

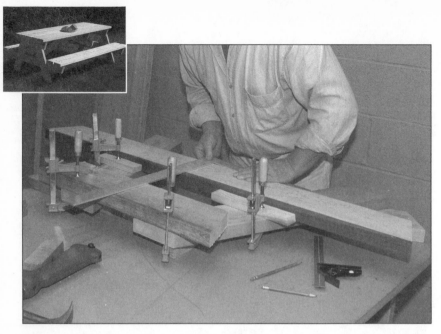

Set up one end. Clamp the top beam to the legs and clamp two scraps at the height of the bench beam, as shown in the drawing below. Square center lines across the top beam and bench beam in order to align them from side to side.

END ASSEMBLY

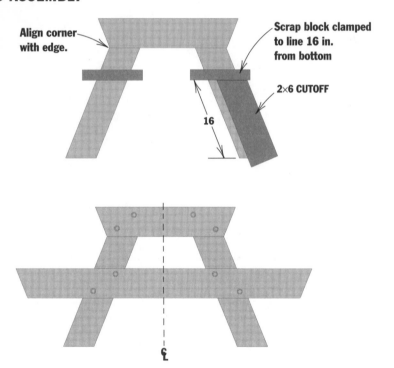

Align corner with edge.

Scrap block clamped to line 16 in. from bottom

2×6 CUTOFF

16

℄

benches. You'll end up with a useful table your family will really enjoy—an indestructible kind of heirloom.

The table will, however, be heavy. It will take two strong men to move it—unless you also make the table truck shown on page 35. Then you can lift one end and roll it away.

This picnic table is made of 2×6 construction lumber, bolted together. It pays to take the time to choose the cleanest material

you can. You don't have to find knot-free wood, but do try to avoid splintered edges and long splits. For a 6-foot table, you'll need eight 12-foot planks.

If you want to make an extra-long table, just cut longer benches, top boards and plates. The legs and support beams remain unchanged. For an 8-foot table, buy seven 16-foot planks; for a 10-foot table, buy eight 16-foot planks.

BUILDING THE PICNIC TABLE

1 Crosscut the planks. Construction lumber is heavy, so you can use a helper. It is easiest to work on a chopsaw or a radial-arm saw, but you can get good results with a portable circular saw, too. Crosscut five of the 2×6 planks in half for the top and benches. When you trim the ends, you'll end up with nine boards about 70 inches long and one extra piece of wood.

2 Saw the angled parts. All of the angled parts are sawn at the same miter setting, 22½ degrees. You can get four legs out of one plank, two bench beams out of a second plank, and the two top beams and two stretchers out of a third plank. The half-plank left over from sawing the benches and top is more than enough for the plates.

3 Set up one end. A table end consists of two legs, a top beam and a bench beam. The strategy is to clamp these parts together, then drill bolt holes. The miters determine the location of the parts. Start by laying both legs flat on the worktable. Set the top beam in position across the legs. The short points of the miters line up with the outside edges of the legs. Locate the bench beam by measuring up 16 inches, then draw lines parallel to the ground. The easiest way to do this is with a mitered 2×6 offcut, as shown in the illustrations on the facing page. Clamp scraps of wood on these lines, and set the bench beam on the scrap blocks. Square a centerline across the top beam and the bench beam so you can align them end to end. Clamp everything together.

Join the legs and beams. With the end assembly clamped together and propped up on scraps, drill through both parts at once. The bolts will be a tight fit, so tap them home with a hammer.

4 Join the legs and beams. The connectors are ⅜-inch galvanized hex-head bolts, with a washer under each head and another washer under the nut. Two bolts go through each joint, separated for maximum triangulation, as shown in the drawing at left. Use scraps of 2×6 to block the assembly up off the worktable. Drill two ⅜-inch holes through both parts of each joint. Tap the bolts into the holes with a hammer, and tighten the nuts down with a socket wrench. You should be able to hear the washers bite into the wood.

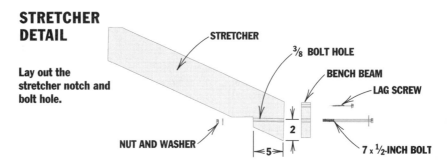

Join the stretchers. Grab the stretcher in a vise to saw the notch (left). Clamp the stretcher flat on the bench to drill the bolt hole (right).

5 Join the stretchers. The angled stretchers brace the tabletop to the bench beams. They're held in place with bolts and lag screws, which might seem like overkill until the first time you drag the table across an uneven deck or patio. In this step you'll join an angled stretcher to each of the end assemblies, then in the next step you'll connect the stretchers with the two plates.

Begin by drilling a ½-inch hole through the center of the bench

STRETCHER DETAIL

Lay out the stretcher notch and bolt hole.

STRETCHER

⅜ BOLT HOLE

BENCH BEAM

LAG SCREW

NUT AND WASHER

2

5

7 x ½-INCH BOLT

beam, 2 inches up from the beam's bottom edge. Then lay out the notch and bolt hole in the stretcher, as shown in the drawing below. Note that the hole is square to the mitered end of the stretcher. Saw the notch

first, then clamp the stretcher flat on the worktable to drill the hole. Bolt the stretcher to the bench beam. Drill pilot holes and install the 3½-inch lag screw. Join the other stretcher and bench beam in the same way.

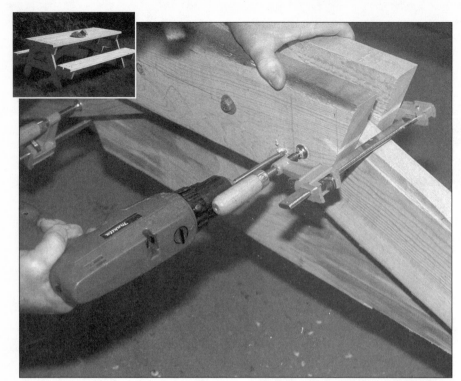

Connect the table ends. Clamp a length of scrap lumber to the two stretchers, and bring their miters together. Clamp the plates to the stretcher joint and drill for bolts (left). Saw the protruding miter points off the stretchers (above).

6 Connect the table ends. The stretchers, joined to each other by the two plates, connect the two ends of the picnic table. Bring the mitered ends of the stretchers together and clamp them to a length of scrap lumber to hold them in position; you can see this piece of scrap below the plates in the photo above. To align the plates with the top beams, stand two of the top boards across the top beams, and bring the plates up to them. Clamp the plates to the stretchers. Now you can drill through the plates and stretchers for four $\frac{3}{8}$-inch bolts. Finally, saw or rasp the protruding miter points off the stretchers, creating a level support for the tabletop.

7 Attach the benches and top. Lag screws, two through each end of every board, connect the bench and top boards to the table frame. Four more screws go through the center top board

Attach the benches and top. Set the top and bench boards in position to lay out holes for lag screws. Drill countersink holes for the bolt heads and washers.

into the stretcher plates. Lay out all the holes. Drill the $\frac{3}{4}$-inch countersink holes first. Then drill $\frac{1}{4}$-inch clearance holes through all the boards. Set the boards in position on the table frame to transfer the locations of these holes. Then remove the

boards in order to drill $\frac{1}{8}$-inch pilot holes into the table frame. Drive all the lag screws home.

8 Finish the table. The best finish for a picnic table is no finish. Let the weather take care of it. The next best is paint.

TABLE TRUCK

Without a table truck, you'd need two strong men to move a heavy picnic table across the lawn. This handy contraption allows one person to move a heavy table unaided. It jacks under the bench beam at one end, then you lift the other end and roll the table away. With two trucks, one person could move the heaviest picnic table without any lifting at all.

The table truck consists of short lengths of 2×4 glued and screwed together, with a pair of ⅜-inch hex-head bolts in the center. The bolts resist the stress of jacking up the table. The longest part is 18 inches, so you might be able to get everything out of scrap. If not, you'll need 12 feet of 2×4.

Set the two rear pillars on the worktable and lay two beams across them. Drill clearance holes, spread glue, and drive four 2½-inch screws into each intersection.

Turn the assembly over, center the front pillar on it, drill bolt holes and start the ⅜-inch bolts. Create clearance by slipping an extra washer onto each bolt between the beams and pillar.

Saw a ½-inch deep groove lengthwise in the face of the axle beam for the 24-inch threaded rod. Saw the groove so the threaded rod fits tightly in it. Now fit the axle and screw the axle beam to the ends of all three pillars.

The handles and tongue give you leverage for jacking up the table. Glue and screw the handles to the tongue, then screw the assembly to the front pillar.

To mount the wheels, tighten a nut and washer onto each end of the axle. Add a washer, then the wheel, then another washer, and finally a pair of nuts.

Rock the table truck under one end of the table, then lift the other end and roll.

TABLE TRUCK

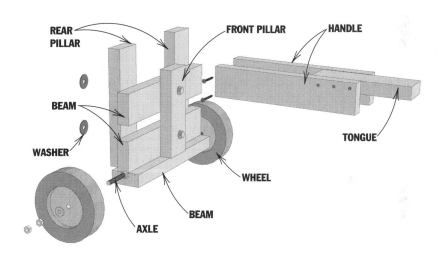

REAR PILLAR — FRONT PILLAR — HANDLE — BEAM — WASHER — WHEEL — BEAM — AXLE — TONGUE

YOUR INVESTMENT
<u>Time:</u> One evening
<u>Money:</u> $20

SHOPPING LIST
12 feet 2×4
Two 8-inch replacement lawn mower wheels
One 24-inch × ½-inch threaded rod
Six ½-inch nuts and washers
Two ⅜ × 3½-inch bolts with nuts and washers

CUTTING LIST

PART	QTY.	DIMENSIONS	NOTES
Beam	3	1½ × 3½ × 18	2×4
Rear pillar	2	1½ × 3½ × 14	2×4
Front pillar	1	1½ × 3½ × 10½	2×4
Handle	2	1½ × 3½ × 18	2×4
Tongue	1	1½ × 3½ × 12	2×4

PARK BENCH

Seat and back slope comfortably, with no angles to cut

The classic park bench has a wooden seat and back, set into one-piece ends made of wrought iron or reinforced concrete. This is an economical and durable civic construction, yet one that permits a surprising amount of comfort. Who doesn't enjoy a rest, or a little snooze, on a park bench?

This park bench, which is made entirely of 2×4 lumber, relies on glued-and-screwed end assemblies. All the pieces are simple rectangular lengths

of 2×4. The design achieves the seat and back slopes necessary for comfort without sawing any angles, as you'll see in the illustrations and in the steps that follow.

The critical maneuver is making sure you construct mirror-imaged end assemblies. One is right-handed and the other is left-handed. Therefore, make the end assemblies in stages, so you can compare them as you go. You'll see this method in the construction photos.

The bench shown here is 60 inches long. You could shorten it to 48 inches, or lengthen it to about 72 inches, without having to make any structural changes. A longer bench would benefit from a second pair of cross rails, plus a brace inside each back leg.

Some of the edges have been rounded over with a router, and some have been left square, to retain the classic park bench look. You can rout as many edges as you like.

BUILDING THE PARK BENCH

1 Choose and saw the wood. You can saw all of the 2×4 lumber to length at the beginning of the project, except for the stretcher. It has to be trimmed to length after the rest of the bench has been assembled. Try to choose clean wood, working around knots and defects. Make sure none of your seat and back slats have pitch pockets.

2 Join the sloper to the back leg. The sloper gives the back slats the tilt they need for comfort. The angle comes from the size and arrangement of the square-cut pieces, not from a protractor. The drawing below shows how the sloper fits diagonally on the back leg. If you match up the sloper's top front corner with the top front corner of the back leg, and allow the sloper's bottom back corner to touch the front edge of the leg, you've got it right. Draw a layout line, spread glue, clamp the parts

PARK BENCH

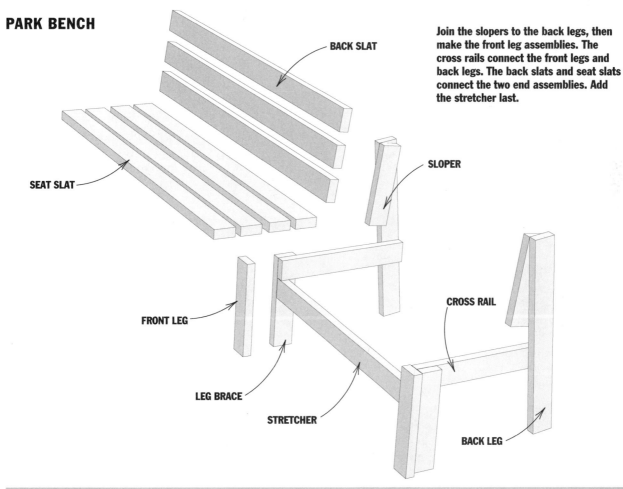

Join the slopers to the back legs, then make the front leg assemblies. The cross rails connect the front legs and back legs. The back slats and seat slats connect the two end assemblies. Add the stretcher last.

YOUR INVESTMENT
Time: One afternoon
Money: $15

SHOPPING LIST
Six 8-foot 2x4 studs
#8 × 2½-inch galvanized screws
#8 × 3-inch galvanized screw

PROJECT SPECS
The park bench is 60 inches long, 32 inches high and 28 inches wide at the ground.

CUTTING LIST

PART	QTY.	DIMENSIONS	NOTES
Back leg	2	1½ × 3½ × 32	2×4
Sloper	2	1½ × 3½ × 14	2×4
Front leg	2	1½ × 3½ × 16½	2×4
Cross rail	2	1½ × 3½ × 24	2×4
Leg brace	2	1½ × 3½ × 16	2×4
Back slat	3	1½ × 3½ × 60	2×4
Seat slat	4	1½ × 3½ × 60	2×4
Stretcher	1	1½ × 3½ × 46	2×4; cut to fit

Join the sloper to the back leg. Fit the sloper diagonally at the top of the back leg and roll glue onto both pieces (above). Clamp them together to drive the screws (right).

Join one front leg and cross rail. Prop the cross rail up on sticks to create the inset, and mark where it meets the front leg (above). Drive the screws toenail fashion, for maximum strength (below).

together, drill clearance holes for four 2½-inch screws and drive the screws down tight. Join the other sloper and back leg in the same way, but be sure you get a right-handed and a left-handed assembly. You can see this relationship in the large photo on the facing page.

3 Join one front leg and cross rail. The front leg connects to the end grain of the cross rail, making a right angle. Even though it's made with three of the 3-inch screws, this is not a secure joint until you've added the leg brace in the next step. Of course the bench has two front legs, but since it's critical to end up with a right-handed and a left-handed assembly, it's best to complete one before beginning the other. Lay the cross rail flat on the worktable and block it up about ³⁄₁₆ inch on a couple of scraps of wood. Align the top of the front leg with the top edge of the cross rail as shown in the photo at left, draw a layout line, and drill three clearance holes through the front leg. Then clamp the parts in position and drive the screws.

4 Add the leg brace. The leg brace secures the connection between the front leg and cross rail. It fits flush at the top, but it's inset by ½ inch at the bottom. This inset allows the seat of the bench to slope toward the back. Roll glue onto the edge of the brace that fits against the front leg, and also glue where it fits against the cross rail. Clamp the brace to the leg, drill clearance holes, and drive two of the 2½-inch screws into it through the front face of the leg. Then

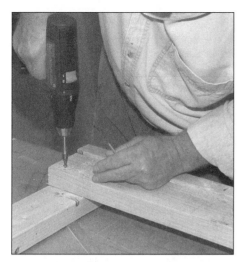

Add the leg brace. Glue and screw the leg brace to the back of the front leg, as well as to the cross rail. Note the ½-inch offset at the bottom of the brace.

END FRAME DETAIL

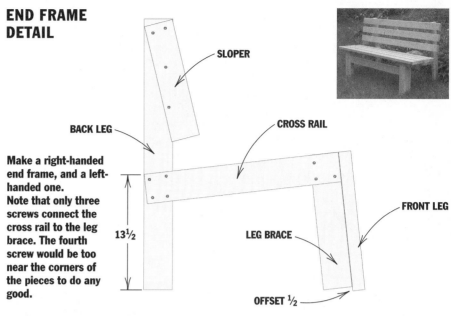

SLOPER

BACK LEG

CROSS RAIL

Make a right-handed end frame, and a left-handed one. Note that only three screws connect the cross rail to the leg brace. The fourth screw would be too near the corners of the pieces to do any good.

13½

FRONT LEG

LEG BRACE

OFFSET ½

Make the second front leg assembly. The second leg assembly matches the first, except one is right-handed and the other is left-handed.

drill and drive three more screws through the cross rail into the brace. Position these screws as shown in the illustration at top right.

5 Make the second front leg assembly. To make the other leg assembly, follow the same sequence as in Steps 3 and 4. However, keep the completed leg assembly close by and make

Join the front and back legs. With the back leg square to the 2×4 that represents the ground, the top of the cross rail is 13½ inches high (above). The cross rail and sloper are on the same side of the leg (right).

sure you end up with a right-handed assembly and a left-handed one, as shown above.

6 Join the front and back legs. The cross rail connects the front leg assembly to the back leg and

The top back slat connects the end assemblies. Clamp the back legs to the worktable to center and attach the top back slat.

Complete the back. Glue and screw the bottom back slat to the sloper.

Make the seat. Center the front seat slat from side to side, overhanging the front leg by 1 inch. Space the other three slats about ¾ inch apart.

sloper. Set the parts up on the worktable as shown in the center photo on the previous page. Clamp one of the seat slats to the edge of the table to represent the ground. Now if you make the back leg vertical, and allow the front leg and brace to both touch the "ground," you'll have created the backward slope of the bench seat. You can verify the slope by direct measurement: Verify that the top of the rail crosses the back leg 13½ inches up from the ground. Draw a layout line, spread glue, drill four clearance holes and drive the 2½-inch screws. Join the other end of the bench in the same way, using the first one as a guide to make sure you end up with mirror-image assemblies.

7 **The top back slat connects the end assemblies.** Set the two end assemblies up on the worktable. Clamp the back legs to the table, 48 inches apart from outside to outside, as shown in the photo above left. If you don't have a big worktable (page 98), you'll have to set up on the floor or on the edge of your deck. Center the top back slat from side to side, and make it flush with the top of the sloper and back leg. Glue and screw the top back slat to the sloper with the 2½-inch screws.

8 **Complete the back.** Center, glue and screw the bottom back slat to the sloper, followed by the middle back slat. The bottom slat overlaps the end of the sloper by about ¼ inch. Center the middle slat in the space between the top and bottom slats.

Add the stretcher. Fit the stretcher into the socket formed by the front leg, leg brace and cross rail. Screw it to the front leg (above). Screw into the stretcher through the leg brace (right).

9 **Make the seat.** To attach the seat slats, turn the bench upright. The front seat slat, which is centered from side to side, overhangs the front leg by 1 inch. Drill clearance holes and drive four of the 3-inch screws down through the front seat slat and into each front leg assembly. Space the remaining three seat slats ¾ inch apart. Drill and drive two 3-inch screws through each end of each slat and into the cross rail below.

10 **Add the stretcher.** The stretcher is a cut-to-fit length of 2×4 that connects the front legs, underneath the seat and cross rail. If you turn the bench upside-down on the worktable, you'll see how it drops neatly into place. Mark and cut the stretcher to length, spread glue where it overlaps the front legs and cross rails, and drive two 2½ inch screws from each direction.

Finish the bench. Rout or rasp the corners off the bottom of the legs, for easy dragging. Also round the front edge of the seat, and the top edge of the back.

11 **Finish the bench.** Forest-green paint is the traditional park-bench finish. To prepare for finishing, fit a roundover cutter in the router and smooth off selected edges. Round the bottom of the legs, to prevent splintering during dragging across the patio. Round the front edge of the seat, and the top of the back. Unless you want a mushy appearance, don't round the ends of the slats. Sand the sharpness off them with 100-grit paper, but leave them crisp. Fill the screw heads with two-part wood putty, and sand all the flat surfaces smooth, and you're ready to prime and paint.

BATTEN PLANTER
This tall box has style and function

Pansies and other cheery little flowers bring more pleasure when they're lifted off the ground and up to where you can see and touch them. This is the purpose of the simple batten planter. It's a quick project you can nail together in a short evening, but you do need to be able to saw wood to width.

The batten planter was designed to hold flats of such flowers as pansies or petunias. The platform can be lowered to house any plant in a clay pot or a plastic bucket. The planter is not, however, designed to be filled with earth. For that, you would need something stronger, like the box planter on page 44.

A batten is a strip of wood that reinforces a joint. In this planter, as in board-and-batten siding, the battens not only conceal the joints, but also give the design a strong vertical rhythm.

BUILDING THE PLANTER

1 Crosscut the parts. Saw four 23-inch lengths of 1×6 pine lumber for the legs and battens, and eight 19-inch lengths for the side panels. Try to work around knots, and keep the scrap for the plant platform.

2 Rip the parts. The parts are not all standard widths of lumber. With the tablesaw, rip or saw lengthwise a 1¼-inch leg

strip off each of the four 23-inch blanks. Measure the remaining width of wood and set the saw to split it in half, so you end up with four wide legs and four battens. Next, saw four of the 19-inch panel blanks to the narrow width of 4¾ inches, and keep the scrap for ledgers. Finally, crosscut the four bat-

tens to the same length as the side panels.

3 Nail the four legs. Use the 2-inch nails to join the four pairs of legs, as shown in the drawing. Strengthen the construction by angling the nails alternately left and right, dovetail-fashion as shown above (opposite).

Join the two-piece legs, then nail the side panels in pairs, to make box corners. Nail the leg assemblies to the box corners, then join everything together with the four battens. Dovetail nailing strengthens the construction. Tilt the nails alternately left and right.

4 **Nail the box corners.** Nail the four pairs of side panels together so that each corner consists of a wide 5½-inch panel and a narrow 4¾-inch panel, as shown in the drawing. Nail a leg assembly to the outside of each box corner.

5 **Assemble the planter.** Set two corner assemblies face down on top of a center batten. Join the two corner assemblies by nailing them to the batten, with 1½-inch nails. Join the other two corner assemblies in the same way. Complete the planter by fitting and nailing the resulting U-shaped halves together.

6 **Support the plants.** Choose your plants and decide how far down to place their support platform. Measure down a another ¾-inch, and nail the ledger strips inside the planter, on two opposite faces. Finally, hold two pieces of scrap 1×6 across the top of the planter, mark them, and cut them so they will fit inside with about ¼-inch of clearance all around. There's no need to nail them to the ledgers.

7 **Finish the planter.** Pine weathers to a silvery grey. If you prefer, paint or stain the planter.

BATTEN PLANTER

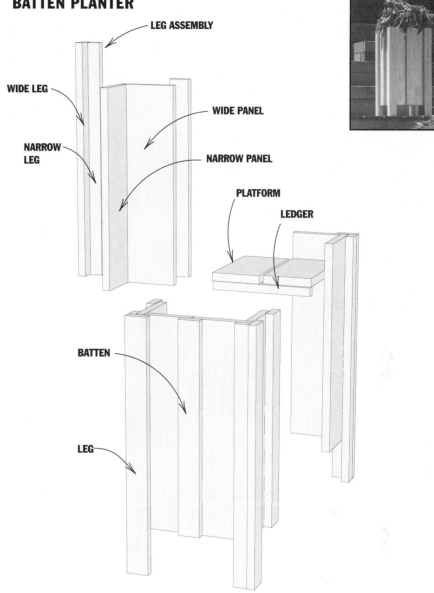

LEG ASSEMBLY

WIDE LEG

NARROW LEG

WIDE PANEL

NARROW PANEL

PLATFORM

LEDGER

BATTEN

LEG

YOUR INVESTMENT
<u>Time:</u> One short evening.
<u>Money:</u> $15

SHOPPING LIST
Three 8-foot lengths of 1×6 lumberyard pine
6d galvanized finishing nails
4d galvanized finishing nails

PROJECT SPECS
The batten planter is 19 inches high, and 12½ inches square.

CUTTING LIST

PART	QTY.	DIMENSIONS	MATERIAL	NOTES
Wide panel	4	¾ × 5½ × 19	5/4 Pine	
Narrow panel	4	¾ × 4¾ × 19	5/4 Pine	
Batten	4	¾ × 2 × 19	5/4 Pine	
Wide leg	4	¾ × 2 × 23	5/4 Pine	
Narrow leg	4	¾ × 1¼ × 23	5/4 Pine	
Ledger	2	¾ × ¾ × 9¼	5/4 Pine	Cut to fit
Platform	2	¾ × 4½ × 9¼	5/4 Pine	Cut to fit

BOX PLANTER

Here's a log cabin you can fill with earth

When you want to fill a deck planter with heavy earth, you need a sturdy box with reinforced corners. This handsome box planter goes together with 2-inch nails, and it's an easy one-evening project. Besides the ability to nail, you need only one skill: sawing wood to length.

The planter sits above the deck on a plinth, which bears all the weight. The plinth improves how the planter looks, and it also makes space for getting a good grip when you want to move your plants around.

The planter shown in the photo was made of 2-inch-wide strips of rough-sawn pine lumber, which measures about an inch thick. You can substitute regular 1×3 or 5/4 × 3 pine from the home center with no change in the cutting list. The only part that would be affected, the corner block, starts out extra long so it can be cut to length toward the end of the project.

We left our planter with no finish, and in time it will weather to a pretty silver-gray. You could paint yours, or stain it, to suit the siding on your house.

BUILDING THE PLANTER

1 Saw the parts. The planter box is made of 20 side rails, which alternate long-short, log-cabin fashion. Saw the 10 long side rails to their final length of 18 inches. Cut the 10 short side

Build a side panel. Nail three long rails to each pair of corner blocks, using another rail to space the parts you are nailing.

rails to 15 inches. They'll be marked and trimmed to final length as you go along. Make the top rails, cap rails, and corner blocks now, too.

2 Build a side panel. One pair of side panels goes short-long-short, while the other pair goes long-short-long. Make a long-short-long panel by nailing three long rails across two corner blocks, leaving spaces for the two short rails. Gauge the spaces with a short rail, as shown in the photo above. Make a second side panel in exactly the same way.

BOX PLANTER

Build the box planter by nailing long side rails to corner blocks. Then fill in the spaces with short side rails. The ledgers connect the planter box to its base.

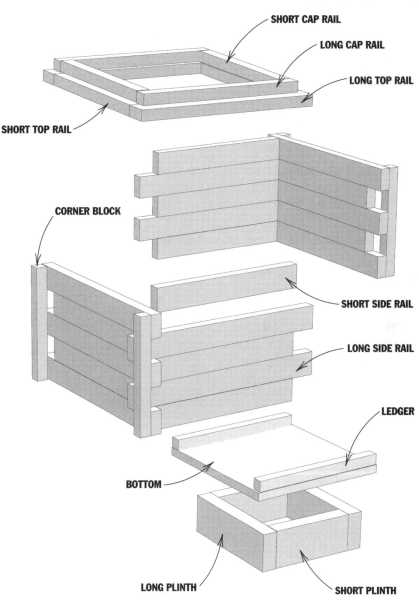

YOUR INVESTMENT

<u>Time:</u> One evening
<u>Money:</u> $15

SHOPPING LIST

32 feet 1×2 rough-sawn pine
4 feet 2×4
13½-inch square of ¾-inch plywood
2-inch galvanized finishing nails
2½-inch galvanized nails
3-inch galvanized nails

PROJECT SPECS

The box planter is 12 inches high, 18 inches wide and 18 inches deep.

CUTTING LIST

PARTS	QTY.	DIMENSIONS	NOTES
Long side rail	10	1 × 2 × 18	
Short side rail	10	1 × 2 × 15	Cut to fit
Corner block	4	1 × 1 × 12	Trim length at end
Long top rail	2	1 × 2 × 18	
Short top rail	2	1 × 2 × 14	Cut to fit
Long cap rail	2	1 × 1¼ × 16¼	
Short cap rail	2	1 × 1¼ × 14	Cut to fit
Ledger	2	1 × 1 × 14	Cut to fit
Long plinth	2	1½ × 3½ × 11⅛	2×4
Short plinth	2	1½ × 3½ × 8⅛	2×4
Bottom	1	¾ × 13½ × 13½	Plywood

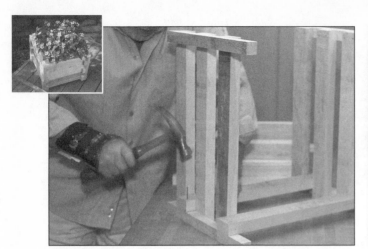

Frame the box. Join the two side panels by nailing long rails into the spaces. Leave the corner blocks extra long until you get the whole planter together.

Fill in the sides. Trim the short rails so they're a tight fit, tap them in place, then nail through the long side pieces into their ends.

3 Frame the box. If you connect these two side panels, you'll have framed out the box. Stand the two side panels up on end, as shown in the photo above. Make sure the corner blocks face outward. Fit a long side rail into the first space. Nail the rail to the corner blocks with two 2-inch finishing nails in each end. Repeat this process to use up all the long side rails. The pieces should fit snugly in their spaces, but not so tightly that you can't easily tap each one into place.

4 Fill in the sides. The short side rails fit into the spaces in the box. They butt tightly against the long side rails, so they need to be trimmed to fit. Hold each rail in place to mark its length, then saw it on the mark. Drive two nails through the long side rail and into the end grain of the short side rail, and so on around the box, until the sides are completely filled in.

5 Complete the top. The top rails and cap rails give a visual finish to the planter. Like the side rails, there are long and short top rails and cap rails. Fit

Join the box and plinth. Drop the plinth and plywood bottom onto the ledgers, and screw the parts together.

the long top rails, then trim the short top rails to fit in between them. Nail these rails in place. Mark and saw the narrower cap rails to frame the box opening, and nail them in place as well.

6 Make the plinth. The plinth, which lifts the box, is made from 2×4 lumber. Crosscut four plinth pieces to the lengths given in the cutting list, and spike them together with 3-inch nails. Drive two nails through the face of the long plinth into the end grain of the short plinth

at each corner. Center the plywood bottom on the plinth and attach it with the 2½-inch nails.

7 Join the box and plinth. The two ledgers connect the planter box to the plywood bottom and to the plinth. Nail the ledgers inside the box, at the top edge of the bottom rail. With the planter upside down on the bench, drop the plywood bottom onto the ledgers and screw the assembly together, as shown above. Your new planter is ready for soil and tomatoes.

PLANT HANGER

Wooden triangle is quick to make

The plastic hangers that come with potted plants look cheesy at best. Sure, everybody plans to repot the fuschias into something nice, with a ropy macramé hanger, but somehow the season flies by before anyone gets around to it. Here's a wooden plant hanger you can get around to making, because it takes hardly any time at all.

The hanger is nothing more than three square sticks of wood, interlaced over-under-over, and held together with a nail or screw through each intersection. A loop of twine around each intersection suspends the device. The size and strength of the nails or screws doesn't mat-ter because they don't bear any weight—they're just locators.

For a 10-inch plant pot, make the sticks 20 inches long and drive the nails or screws 16 inches apart. For an 8-inch pot, make 16-inch sticks and drive the screws 12 inches apart. For other sizes, you can do the geometry if you want, or else you can pin two corners together and fit the sticks around the pot to mark the third intersection.

Cut three pieces of twine twice as long as you want the pot to descend, plus a foot. Double each piece of twine to find its center, then wrap the twine around an intersection of the sticks and knot it, leaving the long ends to dangle. Finally, set the plant in the hanger, bring all six long ends together, and lift the hanger by the twine. Fiddle the twine ends until the plant hangs level, then tie them together with an overhand knot.

YOUR INVESTMENT
Time: 20 minutes
Money: 20 cents

SHOPPING LIST
2 feet 1×4 pine
Ball of twine

PROJECT SPECS
Hangs one 10-inch plant pot.

CUTTING LIST

Part	Qty.	DimensionS	Notes
Rail	3	¾ × ¾ × 20	Fits 10-inch pot

PLANT HANGER

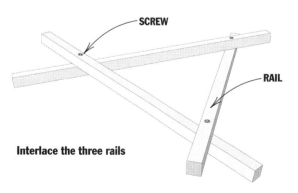

SCREW

RAIL

Interlace the three rails

TEA TIME FOR TOTS

Little suite of chairs and table gives the kids a place to dine or play

Small children need small furniture, and if you spend a lot of time out on your lawn or deck, they will too. This suite of two chairs and a table can be used at mealtime, but it also gives the kids a place to play at having tea, to set up games, and to color or draw. You'll probably bring the suite into the family room for winter play.

All the pieces of wood are rectangular, with no angles to saw anywhere. The construction is completely straightforward glue-and-screw, like most of the pieces in this book. The finished suite can be painted in gay colors, or it can be left to weather.

The design of the chairs and table looks quite interesting as shown, but if you wish to pretty it up you could decorate the sides and back panels as shown on page 55. While you could knock off all the corners and edges with a roundover cutter in your router, doing so would diminish the impact of the design. You can make the wood plenty safe and friendly to the touch with a careful sanding, using 100-grit paper.

CHILD'S CHAIR

CHAIR SIDE

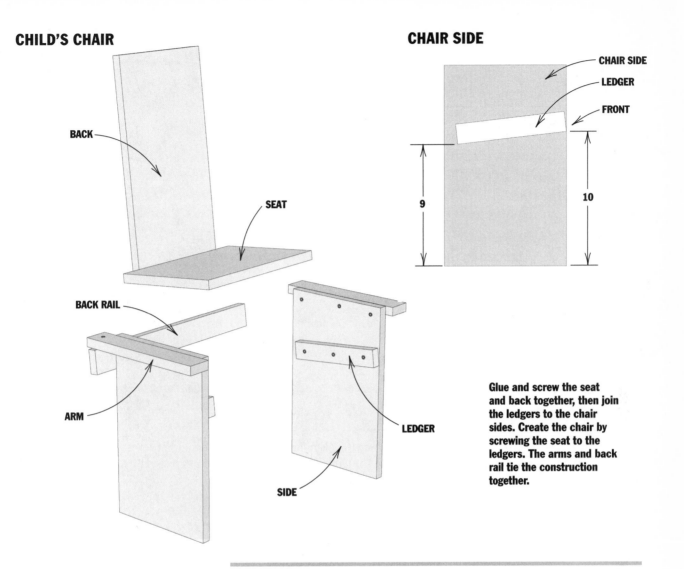

BACK

SEAT

BACK RAIL

ARM

SIDE

CHAIR SIDE

LEDGER

FRONT

9

10

LEDGER

Glue and screw the seat
and back together, then join
the ledgers to the chair
sides. Create the chair by
screwing the seat to the
ledgers. The arms and back
rail tie the construction
together.

BUILDING THE CHILD'S CHAIR

1 Cut the wood. The chair
sides, seat and back are ordinary
1×10 pine lumber, which actually
measures about 9½ inches wide.
The ledgers, arms and rails are
pine 1×2. Saw all the parts except
the arms and back rail to finished
length. Trim the back rail to
length before you screw it to the
chair in Step 6, then trim the
arms flush with the rail in Step 7.
Try to avoid including knots in
any of the chair parts; if you can't
avoid them entirely, organize the
knots into the chair sides instead
of the seat and back.

YOUR INVESTMENT
<u>Time:</u> One afternoon
<u>Money:</u> $8 per chair; $10 per table

PROJECT SPECS
The chair is 27 inches high, 18 inches
wide and 12 inches deep.
The table is 19 inches square
and 16 inches high.

CUTTING LIST

PART	QTY.	DIMENSIONS	NOTES
CHILD'S CHAIR			
Seat	1	¾ × 9½ × 13	1×10 pine
Back	1	¾ × 9½ × 18	1×10 pine
Side	2	¾ × 9½ × 15	1×10 pine
Ledger	2	¾ × 1½ × 8 ½	1×2 pine
Arm	2	¾ × 1½ × 13	1×2; trim to fit
Back rail	1	¾ × 1½ × 19	1×2; trim to fit
CHILD'S TABLE			
Leg	4	¾ × 9½ × 15½	1×10 pine
Top	2	¾ × 9½ × 19	1×10 pine

SHOPPING LIST
CHAIR
6 feet 1×10 pine
6 feet 1×2 pine
TABLE
10 feet 1×10 pine

HARDWARE FOR BOTH
#6 × 1¼-inch galvanized screws
#6 × 2-inch galvanized screws

Join the seat and back. Center the chair back on the edge of the seat, then glue and screw the parts together.

Make the ledgers. Align the ledger so its bottom front corner is flush with the edge of the chair side.

2 Join the seat and back. Draw a centerline on one end of the back, and a centerline on one edge of the seat. Spread glue on the edge of the seat, align the two center marks, and screw through the back and into the edge of the seat with five of the 2-inch screws, as shown in the photo above.

3 Make the ledgers. The ledgers support the seat. They're simple strips of 1×2 glued and screwed to the sides. Draw layout lines on the sides to locate the top of the ledgers, with the front of the line 10 inches up from the floor, and the back of the line 9 inches up. With the top of the ledger on the layout line, its bottom front corner comes flush with the edge of the chair side, as shown in the photo above right. Spread glue, drill clearance holes, and drive three 1¼-inch

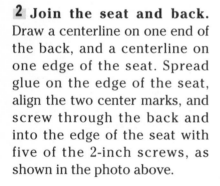

Connect the seat and sides. Clamp the chair seat to the ledger (above), then screw through the side into the seat, and also through the seat into the ledger (right).

screws through each ledger into the side.

4 Connect the seat and sides. The chair seat rests upon the ledgers. The back of the seat sits flush with the back end of the

ledgers. Set the seat in position on one of the ledgers and line it up so you can see where to spread glue. Spread the glue, then clamp the seat to the ledgers, as shown in the photo at left. Drill clearance holes and

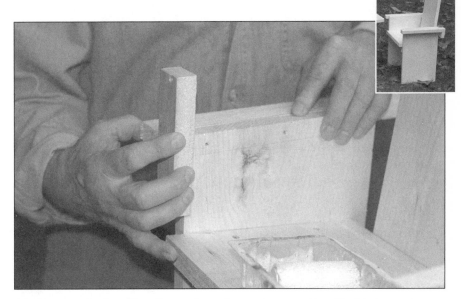

screw through the side into the edge of the seat, using two of the 2-inch screws. Then remove the clamps and screw down through the seat into the ledgers, with the same size screws. Connect the second chair side to the seat in the same way.

5 **Join the arms to the sides.** The arms are pieces of 1×2 attached edge-on to the sides, then tied into the back by the back rail. The offset at the front of the arm is ¾ inch, or the thickness of a piece of scrap, as shown in the photo at right. Spread glue, clamp each arm in place, drill pilot holes and drive three of the 2-inch screws through the chair sides and into each arm.

Join the arms to the sides. Use a piece of scrap to gauge the offset between the chair side and arm. Screw through the side into the arm.

6 **Add the back rail.** The back rail connects the chair arms and supports the back. Hold it in place to mark and saw it to length. Spread glue on the rail, bring it up under the arms, and clamp it flat onto the chair back. Drive three of the 1¼-inch screws through the rail into the chair back. Then drive one 2-inch screw down through each arm into the top of the back rail, as shown in the center photo.

Add the back rail. Screw the back rail to the chair back, then anchor it to the arms.

7 **Finish the chair.** Saw the back end of the arms flush with the back rail. Wrap a piece of 100-grit sandpaper around a block of wood and sand all the sharp edges and corners off the chair. Work over the whole chair, including the bottom of the sides. If you intend to paint the chair, fill in the screw heads with two-part wood putty, let it dry, and sand it flush.

Finish the chair. Saw the extra wood off the back ends of the arms (left). Sand the sharp corners off the wood, making it friendly to the touch (right).

BUILDING THE CHILD'S TABLE

1 Saw the wood. All the parts of the table come out of regular 1×10 pine lumber. Choose the clearest wood for the tabletop.

2 Make the wooden right-angles. The pinwheel base consists of two identical right-angles of wood. Spread glue on the edge of one leg piece, then set a second piece in position on it. Align the edges carefully, as shown in the photo at near right. Then drill clearance holes and make the connection with three 2-inch screws. Make the second L-shape in the same way.

3 Make the pinwheel base. Fit the two wooden right-angles together as shown in far right photo. Draw a layout line, spread glue, then drill clearance holes for 2-inch screws. Drive two screws from each direction.

4 Join the tabletop and base. The two-board tabletop sits on the base at 45 degrees, as shown in the photos below. Position the wood, then connect the parts with two 2-inch screws into each piece of the pinwheel.

5 Finish the table. Sand all the sharp corners off the wood, using a piece of 100-grit sandpaper wrapped around a block of wood. If you want to paint the table, putty the screwheads with two-part wood filler. When the filler dries, sand it flush with the tabletop. Prime the wood before you apply the color coat.

CHILD'S TABLE

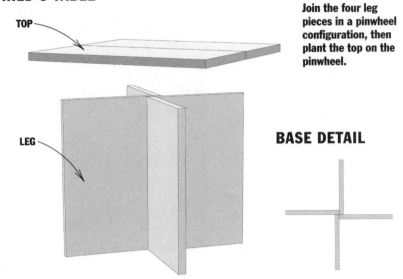

TOP

LEG

Join the four leg pieces in a pinwheel configuration, then plant the top on the pinwheel.

BASE DETAIL

Make the wooden right angles. Prop the leg pieces in position, align them so you can draw a layout line, then glue and screw them together.

Make the pinwheel base. Fit the two wooden right angles together pinwheel fashion, then glue and screw the joint.

Join the tabletop and base. Make a centerline on the edge of the tabletop and align it with the center of the pinwheel (left). Screw the tabletop to the base (right).

ALTERNATIVES

You can dress up the child's table and chairs in any number of ways. The round suite needs a larger tabletop than the square version, 22 inches instead of 19 inches.

Blocks applied to the chair sides can be any shape you like. Instead of blocks, you could make the same shapes as cutouts in the chair sides and back.

Jigsawn shapes lend architectural character to the chairs, as do trim strips.

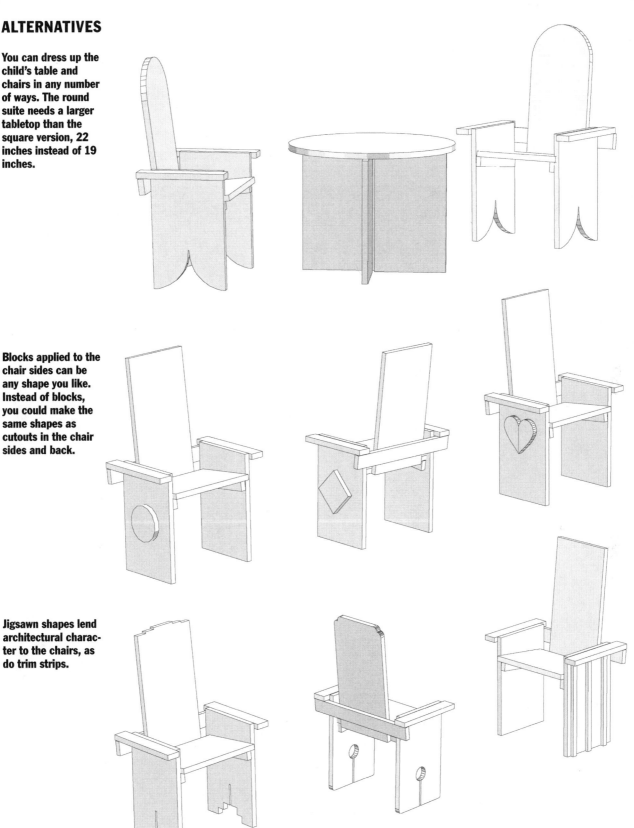

UMBRELLA TABLE

Here's how to make shade while the sun shines

Nothing says summer like an umbrella table with a tray of chilled drinks on it. It makes welcome shade in any climate, and you can always fold the umbrella when you want the full sun.

The design problem is creating enough understructure to support the umbrella, while still leaving some knee room. This handsome table uses a pinwheel construction to accomplish both goals.

The spokes of a pinwheel don't radiate from a common center. Instead, they chase one another around a center space, in this case, a space the size of your umbrella pole. Most sun umbrellas have a 1½-inch pole. Don't guess, however. Measure your umbrella before you construct the table. This dimension also determines the thickness of the legs and the center supports. In the interest of lightness, we made these parts square in section. As an alternative, you could make them of 3-inch-wide wood. This is the width that remains when you saw the rounded edges off a standard 2×4.

Glue and #6 × 2-inch galvanized construction screws are what hold the table structure together. The tabletop is made from ¾-inch pine. It is fastened to the frame with 2-inch galvanized finishing nails. In a high-wind region, there is no way to keep an umbrella table from lifting off the deck, short of nailing it down, so do just that. Drive a nail at an angle through each table leg into the deck itself.

Not only can you choose to make the table legs wider but you also could make all of the parts from thicker wood than the ¾-inch 1×3s and 1×4s shown here.

Make the top pinwheel. Clamp the four long top rails to the umbrella gauge (above). Drill pilot holes, and drive a single screw through the face of each rail into the end of the rail it meets. Remove the clamps and gauge, and turn the assembly over to drive the second screw into each joint (right).

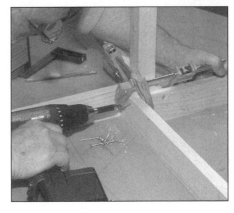

You could substitute 5/4 pine, which finishes around 1⅛ inch thick, without changing any other dimensions. This is because everything follows from the lengths of the parts. The pieces can be wider or thicker without affecting the construction.

BUILDING THE UMBRELLA TABLE

1 Saw the parts. Saw all the wood for the table structure before you begin to build. There are a lot of parts and, confusingly, they are all of similar size, so group them and give each group an identifying mark to help you keep track. You can saw the wood for the tabletop at the same time, or you can leave it to cut to fit at the end. But while you are working at the saw, make a square stick of wood the same dimension as your umbrella pole. It will be the gauge piece around which you assemble the table framework.

2 Make the top pinwheel. The core of the table structure is a pair of pinwheels. Start by clamping the four top rails to the umbrella gauge piece, as shown in the top photo. Check for square, then drill pilot holes and drive one screw through the face of each top rail and into the end grain of the next rail around the pinwheel. Remove the clamps and turn the assembly over on the worktable. Drill pilot holes and drive a second screw through each joint. For the strongest joints, angle the screws. Join the four bottom rails into a second pinwheel in exactly the same way.

UMBRELLA TABLE

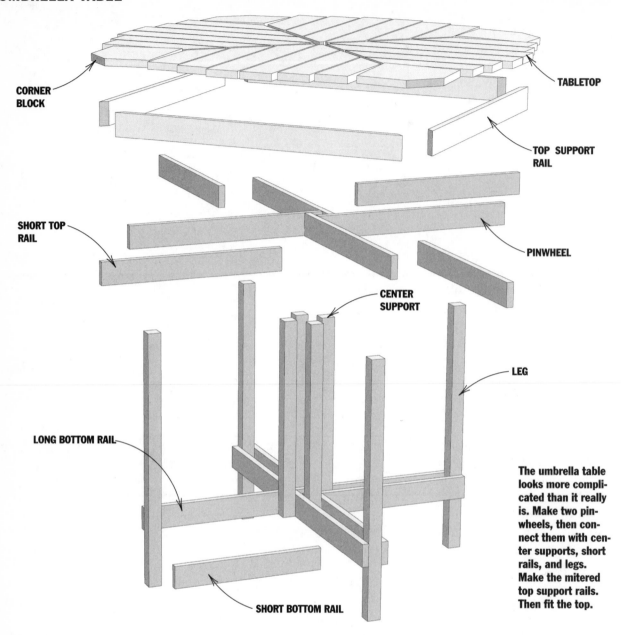

CORNER BLOCK

TABLETOP

TOP SUPPORT RAIL

SHORT TOP RAIL

PINWHEEL

CENTER SUPPORT

LEG

LONG BOTTOM RAIL

SHORT BOTTOM RAIL

The umbrella table looks more complicated than it really is. Make two pinwheels, then connect them with center supports, short rails, and legs. Make the mitered top support rails. Then fit the top.

YOUR INVESTMENT
Time: One weekend
Money: $60

SHOPPING LIST
40 feet 1×3 pine
40 feet 1×4 pine
10 feet 2×4
4 feet 1×12
#6 × 2-inch galvanized screws
2-inch galvanized finishing nails

PROJECT SPECS
The table is 29 inches high. The top is 48 inches across.

CUTTING LIST

PART	QTY.	DIMENSIONS	NOTES
Long top rail	4	$^3/_4 \times 2^1/_2 \times 23$	1×3
Long bottom rail	4	$^3/_4 \times 2^1/_2 \times 20$	1×3
Center support	4	$1^1/_2 \times 1^1/_2 \times 22$	Cut from 2×4
Short bottom rail	4	$^3/_4 \times 2^1/_2 \times 17^3/_4$	1×3
Leg	4	$1^1/_2 \times 1^1/_2 \times 28$	1×2
Short top rail	4	$^3/_4 \times 2^1/_2 \times 20^3/_4$	1×3
Top support rail	4	$^3/_4 \times 2^1/_2 \times 32$	Miter both ends
TABLETOP			
Corner block	4	$^3/_4 \times 11^3/_8 \times 9^1/_2$	Mitered as shown
Short tabletop	8	$^3/_4 \times 3^1/_2 \times 13$	Miter one end
Long tabletop	8	$^3/_4 \times 3^1/_2 \times 17^1/_2$	Miter one end
Center tabletop	8	$^3/_4 \times 3^1/_2 \times 22^1/_4$	Double miter

3 Add the center supports.

The four center supports connect the two pinwheels, as shown in the illustration below, but as a first step just join them onto the top wheel. Begin with one center support. Set it on the edge of the worktable, then position the pinwheel on it, as shown in the top left photo. Draw layout lines so you can spread glue on the mating surfaces, then clamp the assembly together. Drill pilot holes. Drive two screws through the face of the rail and into the center support. Drive a third screw into the support from inside the pinwheel center. Bury the screw head in the wood. Join the other three center supports to the wheel in the same way.

4 Connect the pinwheels.

The second pinwheel should plug right onto the free end of the four center supports. If the pinwheel seems as if it can't possibly fit, it's upside-down. When you get it right, draw layout lines so you can spread glue, then clamp the whole assembly together. It will take eight clamps to bring all the mating surfaces tightly together. Measure the distance between each pair of top and bottom rails to make sure the two pinwheels are parallel to one

Add the center supports. Glue and clamp the pinwheel to the first center support, so you can drill pilot holes and screw the parts together (left). Rotate the assembly to add center supports. Support the free end of the top rail with a block of scrap, as at left in the photo above.

Connect the pinwheels. Spread glue, plug the two assemblies together, and clamp them. Measure the height at the ends of the rails to make sure the two pinwheels are parallel (left). Drill pilot holes and screw through the rails into the center supports (right).

PINWHEEL CONNECTION

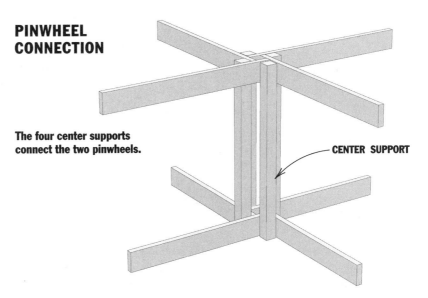

The four center supports connect the two pinwheels.

CENTER SUPPORT

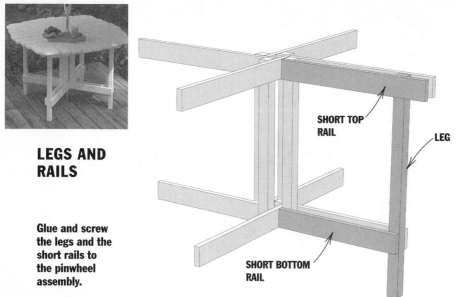

LEGS AND RAILS

Glue and screw the legs and the short rails to the pinwheel assembly.

SHORT TOP RAIL

LEG

SHORT BOTTOM RAIL

Connect the mitered rails. Clamp each mitered top support rail against the top rails. The clamps won't slip if you position them as shown here. Glue and screw the support rails in place. Set the screws an inch back from the end of the rails.

Lay out the top. Tack-nail the ½-inch spacer gauge strips to the table base. Make sure the strips are square to each other and to the top support rails.

another. Drill pilot holes and drive two screws through each joint. Always drive the screws through the rail and into the wood of the center support.

5 Add the legs and rails. Glue, clamp, and screw a leg to the assembled pinwheels, then remove the clamps to glue and screw the short rails in place. The illustration at left shows how these parts fit together. You can make the joints tight and accurate, but only if you take the time to draw layout lines, spread glue, and clamp. Drill pilot holes and drive two screws through each joint, then unclamp the assembly in order to drive another pair of screws into the joint from the other side. Rotate the table base on the worktable to add the remaining three legs and all the rest of the rails.

6 Miter the top support rails. The four top support rails not only support the tabletop boards but they also tie the table base tightly together. Start by mitering one end of each support rail at 45°. Stand the assembled base upright on the floor. Hold the rails in position to mark and cut the remaining miters.

7 Connect the mitered rails. The mitered rails should fit tightly between the arms of the leg-and-rail assemblies. Spread glue on the face of the miters, then clamp the first support rail in position. Drill pilot holes for two galvanized screws in each end, and drive the screws home. Start the screws about an inch back from the ends of the rails, so they bite through the full thickness of the wood.

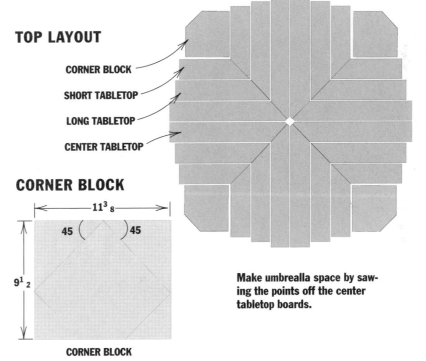

Fit the top boards. Starting with the center boards and working one section at a time, fit the tabletop together (left). Space the boards with the narrow gauge strips and nail them to the table structure (right).

8 Lay out the top. The tabletop is a herringbone pattern of 1×4 boards. The corners are filled in with five-sided corner blocks sawn from a 1×12 board. Start at the center of each section, and work out toward the corner blocks. To begin, saw two pairs of spacer gauge strips. One pair is ½ inch thick, and the other is ¼ inch thick. Tacknail the thick gauge strips to the table frame, as in the bottom photo at left.

9 Fit the top boards. Crosscut all the top boards to the lengths given in the cutting list, and miter them all. Nip ½ inch off the point of the eight center boards, so they'll clear the umbrella opening. Set two center boards against the gauge strips. Butt the miters together. Nail the center boards to the table structure with the 2-inch finishing nails. Work toward the corners, spacing the boards with the ¼-inch gauge strips and nailing them to the structure. Fill in the other three sections in the same way.

TOP LAYOUT

CORNER BLOCK

SHORT TABLETOP

LONG TABLETOP

CENTER TABLETOP

CORNER BLOCK

$11^3\!/\!_8$

45   45

$9^1\!/\!_2$

CORNER BLOCK

Make umbrealla space by sawing the points off the center tabletop boards.

10 Fit the corner blocks. The corner blocks have five sides, but they're made by cutting a series of miters, as shown in the drawing above. Begin by crosscutting four 9½-inch lengths off the 1×12 board. Draw a centerline and saw a miter both ways from this center point. Finally, make square cuts from the ends of the miters. The corner blocks should neatly fill the corner spaces. Nail them to the frame.

11 Finish the table. To make your umbrella table friendly to the touch, sand a small flat on all the exposed edges. Sand all the surfaces as well, with 80-grit and 120-grit paper. Now you can paint the table, varnish it, or leave it alone to weather.

Deck Tables

Here's a simple and versatile design you can vary to suit your own needs

For real outdoor comfort, you need the same pieces of furniture as indoors. Where there are chairs, you also need tables. Here is a versatile design for a small table, which can be made in various heights and lengths.

Even though this is a simple construction, the results don't look simple. This makes it an interesting first project. You'll learn the fundamental techniques of sawing a square end on the wood and also of sawing a miter. You'll also learn about gluing and nailing, and clamping to a gauge to make identical assemblies.

The instructions include dimensions for two sizes of table. One is small and low, like a little bench, while the other is taller and somewhat more robust, like an end table. The low table goes together with siding nails and glue. The end table goes together with screws and glue—its parts are included in the cutting list, and there's more detail about making it on page 63. You can see how straightforward it is to tailor this table design to your own purposes.

YOUR INVESTMENT

Time: Two tables in an evening.
Money: Low table, $8. End table, $12.

SHOPPING LIST

LOW TABLE
12 feet 1×6 pine
4 feet 1×4 pine
2½-inch galvanized siding nails

PROJECT SPECS

The low table measures 16¾ inches high, 24 inches long, and 11½ inches wide. The end table measures 23¾ inches high, 24 inches long, and 15 inches wide.

END TABLE
8 feet 1×8 pine
8 feet 1×6 pine
4 feet 2×4 stud
#6 × 2-inch galvanized screws
#8 × 2½-inch galvanized screws

CUTTING LIST

PART	QTY.	DIMENSIONS	NOTES
LOW TABLE			
Leg	4	¾ × 5½ × 16	1×6 pine
Shelf	2	¾ × 3½ × 16	1×4; miter both ends 45°
Top	2	¾ × 5½ × 24	1×6 pine
END TABLE			
Leg	4	¾ × 7½ × 23	2×8 pine
Shelf	2	1½ × 3½ × 20	2×4; miter both ends 45°
Top	3	¾ × 4½ × 28	1×5 pine

LOW TABLE

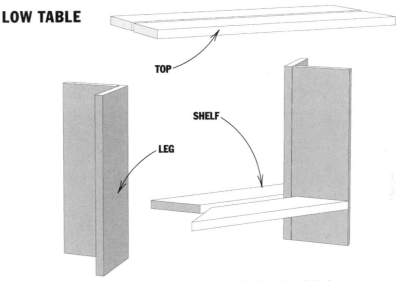

TOP

SHELF

LEG

Make two wooden right angles and connect them with the mitered shelves. Then add the top. Tailor the dimensions to suit yourself.

LEG ASSEMBLY

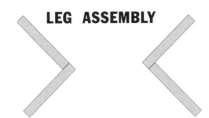

BUILDING THE LOW TABLE

1 Saw the wood. The table parts come out of standard widths of pine lumber. If you've already been building projects around the house and yard, you've probably got a stack of salvageable short ends.

2 Assemble the legs. Each of the two leg assemblies is a wooden right-angle made by gluing and nailing two identical boards together. As shown in the photo at right, you can use one set of parts to prop up the ones you're working on. Spread glue on the edge of one board, and start three 2½-inch siding nails near the edge of the other.

Assemble the legs. Glue and nail two leg pieces together, forming a right angle (above). Scrape excess glue off the wood while it's still wet. Use a chisel or a putty knife (right).

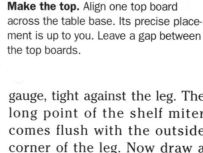

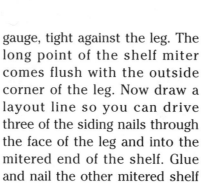

Join the shelves to one leg assembly. Clamp a gauge block to the leg, spread glue on the mitered end of the shelf, then clamp it to the gauge (left). Nail through the leg into the mitered end of the shelf (above).

Join the second leg assembly to the shelves. Spread glue on the miters and fit them around the second leg assembly. Nail the parts together.

Make the top. Align one top board across the table base. Its precise placement is up to you. Leave a gap between the top boards.

Line the pieces up as best you can, then drive one nail home. Check the alignment before you drive the other two nails. Assemble the other two leg pieces in exactly the same way.

3 Join the shelves to one leg assembly. The shelves connect the leg assemblies and stiffen the construction. To make a gauge for locating the shelves on the legs, find or cut a scrap of shelf material. Clamp it to one leg, as shown in the photo top left. The gauge establishes a temporary reference surface that's parallel to the ground. Roll glue onto the mitered end of the shelf, and clamp it to the

gauge, tight against the leg. The long point of the shelf miter comes flush with the outside corner of the leg. Now draw a layout line so you can drive three of the siding nails through the face of the leg and into the mitered end of the shelf. Glue and nail the other mitered shelf to the same leg assembly in the same way.

4 Join the second leg assembly to the shelves. The free ends of the mitered shelves make a vee-shape, into which you can plug the second leg assembly. Note, however, that by turning the second leg assembly upside down, you've

got a choice between two orientations, so choose the one shown in the drawing on page 61. Clamp the gauge across the leg, and spread glue on the two mitered shelf ends. Rest the shelves on the gauge and push the miters tight against the leg assembly, then clamp the shelves to the gauge. Now you can nail through the legs into the mitered ends of the shelf, as you did at the other end of the table.

5 Make the top. The tabletop consists of two boards nailed to the legs, with a gap in between them. Center the top boards on the legs, and decide on the width of gap you like. Then nail both boards down, with three nails into the end of each leg.

6 Finish the table. You can paint the table to match other outdoor furniture, or you can stain it to match your house, or you could varnish it to show off the wood. However, if you don't do anything, it will be OK. The wood soon will weather to a soft gray.

END TABLE

The end table is a larger and more robust version of the low table. Although its construction is the same, the parts are bigger, and the shelf is made of 2×4 instead of 1×4. This creates a broader shoulder of wood to resist racking stress. The addition of a third board to the table-top introduces an additional complication, which is discussed below.

Since glue and screws hold the end table together, you have to drill clearance holes. The purpose of a clearance hole is to make an easy path for the screw through the first piece of wood, plus a starting hole in the second piece. Even with clearance holes, you must hold the wood tightly together when you drive the screws, and it's best to clamp it.

When you screw a pair of leg pieces together, making a wooden right-angle, you can improve the alignment of the joint if you make it in stages. Spread the glue, align the parts, drill the first clearance hole and drive the first 2½-inch screw. Then check the alignment and adjust it if necessary before you drill clearance holes for the remaining two or three screws.

Screws also join the mitered 2×4 shelves to the leg assemblies. Use a gauge to position the shelf parts, as discussed in Steps 3 and 4 on the previous page. Trace the outline of the mitered shelf onto the leg pieces. Then drill each pilot hole twice, once from each side of the wood, instead of just from one side. This eliminates a little divot of wood, caused by the drill, that might otherwise interfere with a good connection. Drive four 2-inch screws into each miter, and don't forget the glue.

The top of the end table consists of three identical boards nailed to the legs. Because of the way you made the right-angle leg assemblies,

however, the table base is not a symmetrical construction. Draw a center line on the underside of the top center board. Then stand the table base upside-down on this board. You'll be able to see how to balance the base and top. Mark where the base meets the edges of the center board, so you can put the parts back in position right-side up. Nail or screw down through the center board into the ends of the legs. Now position the other two top boards alongside the center board, and attach them in the same way.

End table. The table has a space between its mitered shelves.

Use a gauge block to locate and support the 2x4 shelf.

Drill pilot holes for the screws. Drill from both sides of the wood.

Stand the table base upside-down on the top center board and balance its location. Draw layout lines so you can attach the top center board to the base.

PLANT POST

A skyhook for baskets of flowers

Hanging baskets of impatiens, fuschias or begonias are delightful, but what if there's nowhere to hook them? This plant post is a freestanding column you can nail to your deck or stake in the garden. It has eight hooks from which to hang your favorite flowering plants.

The post's construction creates interesting patterns of shadows that change as the sun moves. The base and top construction looks like intricate wooden joints, but it's just simple pieces of wood glued and nailed together. The key is always to bridge two short pieces of wood with a long piece.

We built our post out of 1-inch rough-sawn pine lumber. You can substitute regular 1× (¾-inch) pine, or 5/4 pine, if you prefer, as long as all your wood is the same thickness.

BUILDING THE POST

1 Cut all the parts. Rough-sawn 1×6 pine measures close to 6 inches wide, but 1×6 pine from the home center, which has been planed smooth, measures about 5½ inches wide. Rough or smooth, by carefully sawing lengthwise, you can get a wide flat piece and a narrow

PLANT POST

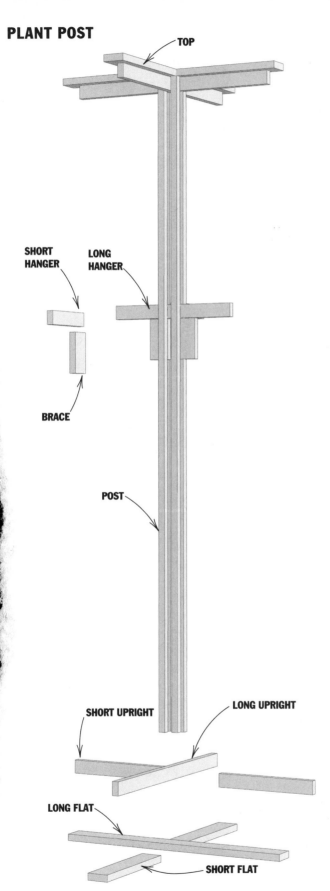

TOP

SHORT HANGER

LONG HANGER

BRACE

POST

SHORT UPRIGHT

LONG UPRIGHT

LONG FLAT

SHORT FLAT

The plant post's cross-shaped top and base are identical. The long flat piece crosses the long upright piece, with the short pieces nailed and glued to this cross.

DETAIL OF BASE AND TOP

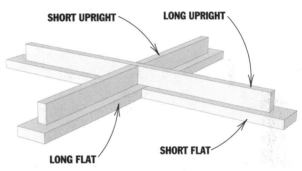

SHORT UPRIGHT

LONG UPRIGHT

LONG FLAT

SHORT FLAT

YOUR INVESTMENT
<u>Time:</u> One afternoon or evening
<u>Money:</u> $15

SHOPPING LIST
24 feet 1×6 rough-sawn pine
2½-inch galvanized spiral nails
3-inch galvanized spiral nails
Eight #6 × 3-inch steel hooks

PROJECT SPECS
The plant post stands 8 feet high and its base is a 36-inch cross.

CUTTING LIST

PART	QTY.	DIMENSIONS
Post	4	1 × 1 × 96
Long flat	2	1 × 3³⁄₁₆ × 36
Long upright	2	1 × 2 × 32
Short flat	4	1 × 3³⁄₁₆ × 16½
Short upright	4	1 × 2 × 15½
Long hanger	1	1 × 2 × 19½
Short hanger	2	1 × 2 × 9⁷⁄₁₆
Brace	4	1 × 3 × 6

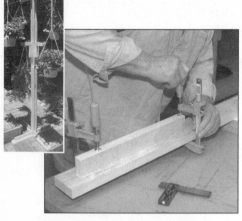

Make half the base. Glue, clamp and nail the first short upright piece to the long flat piece. The short piece is inset 1⅞ inches from the end (above). Reserve a space the thickness of a piece of scrap, and join the other short upright to the base assembly (right).

Complete the base. Glue and nail the long upright into the gap, then join the short flat pieces to the base. Spread the glue with a small paint roller.

upright piece from each length of 1×6 material. The four vertical posts are also sawn out of one 8-foot length of 1×6 lumber. This way they'll all come out exactly the same length.

2 Make half the base. The joints in the cross-shaped base are created by the way you assemble the parts, not by cutting notches or slots. Spread

glue on the edge of one short upright piece, and position it on a long flat piece. Center the upright piece from side to side, but set it 1⅞ inches back from the end of the flat piece. Clamp the two pieces together, then nail through the long flat into the short upright. Use 2½-inch nails. Glue and nail the second short upright piece to the long flat in the same way, but insert a

scrap spacer to create a gap the precise thickness of the wood, as shown in the top right photo.

3 Complete the base. Fit the long upright into the gap you created with the piece of scrap. It should be a tight fit. Center it and check it for square, and twist it into line if necessary, then lock it in place with a pair of 2½-inch nails through the bottom of the long flat piece. Now glue and nail the two short flat pieces onto the assembly. This completes the base.

4 Make the top. The top of the plant post is the same as the base. Glue and nail two long pieces and four short ones together in exactly the same way. Now examine the two cross-shaped assemblies. If one has a flatter bottom side than the other, declare it the base.

5 Join the base and posts. Lay two of the posts across the worktable and plug the base assembly onto them. See where glue should go, and spread the glue. Hold the parts together with spacer blocks and clamps, and check for square as shown in the top left photo on the facing page. Drill a pilot hole and drive a 3-inch spiral nail through the base into the end grain of each post. Nail the posts to the base's upright pieces. Nail the other two vertical posts to the base assembly in the same way.

6 Join the top to the posts. The top assembly plugs directly onto the four posts. Put the parts together dry to see where to spread glue, then take them apart in order to spread it.

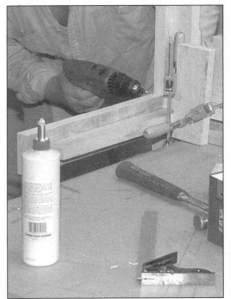

Clamp up, check for square, and nail as in Step 5.

7 Nail the long hanger. The hangers and braces fit into the slots between the posts. Slide the long hanger down to 32 inches from the top and center it from side to side. Nail it to one post, then check for square before nailing it to the other. Glue and nail two braces between the posts, tight under the long hanger.

8 Nail the short hangers. The two short hangers and the two remaining braces fill the remaining spaces between the posts. Spread glue on the braces and hangers before you tap them into place, then nail them tight.

9 Add hooks and plants. Drill $\frac{3}{16}$-inch pilot holes for the hooks in the ends of the top flat pieces and hanger pieces. Twist the #6 hooks into the wood. Now add plants. To keep the post from blowing over, nail the base to the deck, but leave the nailheads sticking up so it's easy to move.

Join base and posts. Clamp two posts to the worktable, then clamp the base assembly to them. Check for square (above). Nail the base to the posts (top right). Blocks of scrap help clamp the second pair of posts to the base. Drill pilot holes and nail through the flat base pieces into the ends of the posts (right).

Nail the short hangers. Fit the last two braces between the posts, then add the short hangers. Nail them to the posts.

Attach the brace. Clamp the brace to the arm and nail into it through both the wall plate and arm.

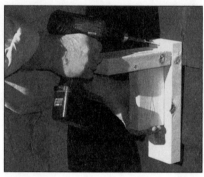

Mount the bracket. Screw the bracket to a stud, through the wall of the garage.

WALL BRACKET

How to get heavy stuff off the ground

A pair of these handy brackets, which you nail together from scraps of 2×4, will support as many as three ladders on the wall of the garage. You can use the brackets for whatever you want to organize and store: lumber, pipes, bicycles, hoses. However, don't make the arm longer than about 12 inches.

BUILDING THE BRACKET

1 Choose the wood. Gather enough 2×4 or 2×6 scrap to make two brackets at a time.

2 Nail the arm to the wall plate. Begin by spiking the arm onto the wall plate with three 3½-inch galvanized spiral nails.

3 Attach the brace. Clamp the brace in position, as shown in the top photo. Drive three spiral nails into the brace through the wall plate, and three more through the arm.

4 Mount the bracket. Screw or nail the brackets to the wall. Be sure the fasteners go into studs.

YOUR INVESTMENT
Time: One hour
Money: $3

PROJECT SPECS
The wall bracket extends 11½ inches out from the wall, and 16 inches down the wall.

SHOPPING LIST
6 feet 2×4 stud
3½-inch galvanized spiral nails

CUTTING LIST

PART	QTY.	DIMENSIONS
Wall plate	2	1½ × 3½ × 16
Arm	2	1½ × 3½ × 10
Brace	2	1½ × 3½ × 6

WALL BRACKET

Nail the arm to the wall plate, then nail the brace into position between the arm and wall plate. Make the wall brackets in pairs.

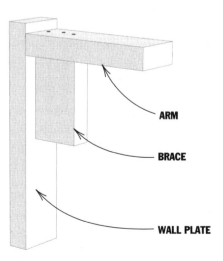

ARM

BRACE

WALL PLATE

LITTLE DECK

Build this flat spot in an afternoon

A little deck gives you a place to park your lawn chair while you watch the kids, or a level barbecue platform on an uneven lawn You could pitch a tent on it, or put up a screen house. There's lots of places to use a little deck in the yard, provided you've got an easy way to make it.

The project results in a 6-foot × 6-foot deck. You can make it larger or smaller, as suits you. It can sit easily on level land, and it's not difficult to stake into a slope. You can build and install this deck in an afternoon.

The deck framework is made of 2×4s spiked together with 4-inch galvanized nails. Although you drill clearance holes, these nails nevertheless require a substantial amount of hammering. As an alternative, you can connect the joists with metal joist hangers. The little deck is small enough to construct inside the workshop, though it might be more convenient to work on the main deck off your house.

The platform is an assembly of four 24-inch × 48-inch pieces of ¾-inch exterior grade plywood, with one 24-inch square of plywood in the center. This not only makes an interesting pattern, it liberates you from wrestling with a 4×8 sheet. Home centers sell half-sheets and quarter-sheets that are accurately cut and easy to carry, for a small price premium.

BUILDING THE DECK

1 Cut the wood. Saw the joists to length at the start of the project. Don't trim the headers to length until you've nailed the joists to the rim joist and can measure the actual spans. The fit should be snug, and it's affected not only by centering the plywood decking, but also by the thickness of the wood.

2 Lay out the rim joists. The four joists run between the two rim joists, which therefore have to be marked out to match one another. Start with two 8-foot studs for rim joists; you'll be able to use the overhang to help you install the deck, and you can saw the excess off at the end, or leave it if you like. Clamp the two rim joists together face-to-face and locate the four joists, as

shown in the top right photo on the facing page. The layout dimension is the width of the 2-foot × 4-foot pieces of plywood. The two outside joists need to be 6 feet apart from outside edge to outside edge. Space the two inside ones 24 inches from outer edge to joist center.

3 Nail the joists to one rim joist. Two of the 4-inch nails, dri-

LITTLE DECK

To make the little deck, spike the joists to the rim joists. Then add the headers. Locate the deck, stake it to the ground, and fit the posts. Deck it with ¾-inch plywood.

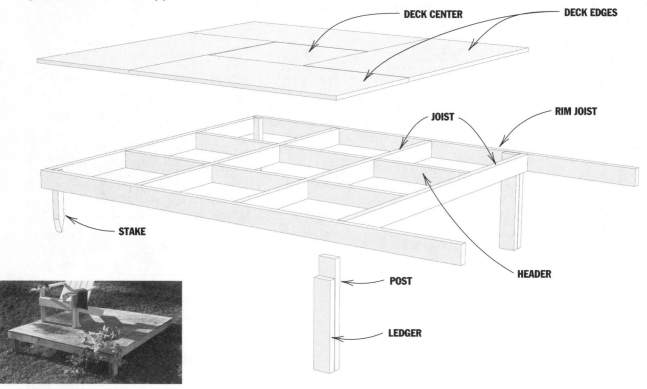

DECK CENTER   DECK EDGES

JOIST   RIM JOIST

STAKE

POST   HEADER

LEDGER

YOUR INVESTMENT

<u>Time:</u> One afternoon.
<u>Money:</u> $50

SHOPPING LIST

Seven 8-foot 2×4
4-inch galvanized nails
#8 × 3-inch galvanized screws
2 ½-inch siding nails

PROJECT SPECS

The little deck is 6 feet square.

CUTTING LIST

PART	QTY.	DIMENSIONS	NOTES
Rim joist	2	$1\frac{1}{2} \times 3\frac{1}{2} \times 96$	2×4
Joist	4	$1\frac{1}{2} \times 3\frac{1}{2} \times 69$	2×4
Header	6	$1\frac{1}{2} \times 3\frac{1}{2} \times 24$	2×4; trim to fit
Stake	2	$1\frac{1}{2} \times 1\frac{1}{2} \times 12$	From 2×4
Post	2	$1\frac{1}{2} \times 3\frac{1}{2} \times 24$	Cut to fit
Ledger	2	$1\frac{1}{2} \times 3\frac{1}{2} \times 24$	Cut to fit
Deck center	1	$\frac{3}{4} \times 24 \times 24$	CDX plywood
Deck edge	4	$\frac{3}{4} \times 24 \times 48$	CDX plywood

Lay out the rim joists. Clamp the rim joists together and locate the four joists. Space them so the plywood decking falls on the joist center lines.

Nail the joists to one rim joist. Drill clearance holes and nail the four joists to one of the rim joists. Drill and nail on an angle to strengthen the joint.

ven through the rim joist into the end grain of each joist, will make a strong connection. Clamp the first joist in position on the worktable and drill two $\frac{3}{16}$-inch clearance holes through the rim joist. Drill the clearance holes so they toe in a few degrees, as shown in the photo above right. Swing the heaviest hammer you can manage to drive the 4-inch nails home. Attach the other three joists to the rim joist in the same way.

4 **Attach the other rim joist.** The second rim joist traps the free ends of the joists. Unless you're working on the floor, by now you will have overflowed the bounds of your worktable. You can support the structure on the table by clamping scrap props to the overhang, as shown in the center photo. Drill the $\frac{3}{16}$-inch clearance holes and nail the rim joist to the free ends of all four joists.

5 **Make the headers.** The six headers make the deck frame into a tic-tac-toe pattern, creating solid support for the plywood. The headers should fit tightly into the joist bays, so measure and cut each pair to fit.

Attach the other rim joist. Clamp props to the construction to support it while you nail the other rim joist to the free ends of the joists (center). Measure the diagonals to make sure the frame is square (above).

Start with the two headers between the two center joists. Use the actual plywood as a gauge to locate and nail the headers in place, as shown in the photo at left. Then nail the remaining headers across the outside joist bays. Make the center connections by toe-nailing, as shown in the center photos.

6 **Locate the deck.** It's much easier to locate and stake the deck to the ground without the plywood decking in place. The best site is dead-level grass, and the next best is a gentle slope. Carry the frame to where you want it and arrange it so one edge, or at least one corner, sits firmly on the ground. With this edge staked, you can raise the other edge onto 2×4 posts, as discussed in Steps 8 and 9.

Make the headers. Cut the two center headers and fit them in place, using the center square of plywood as a gauge (above). Nail the headers to the joists (below left). Toenail the outside headers where they meet the center headers. Toenail through the face of the joist, not through the edge, on the angle indicated by the bit that will drill the clearance hole (below right).

7 **Stake the deck.** Drive a 12-inch stake inside the grounded corner of the deck frame. Drive the stake down below the top of the joists. Drill two clearance holes through the stake, and fas-

Stake the deck. Carry the frame to the site and drive a stake at the high corner (left). Drill clearance holes and drive two screws through the stake into the joists (above).

ten it to the joists with 3-inch screws, as shown in the bottom left photo on the previous page. Move to the next highest corner and block it up level on rocks or bricks. Drive the second stake into the pocket formed by the joists and attach it with two screws. Tamp the supporting rocks firmly under the joist.

8 Pitch the deck. Now move to the free edge of the deck and block it up to about an inch from dead level. This pitch allows it to drain. You can pitch it on stacks of rocks or scrap, or you can clamp props to it, as shown in the photo at top right.

9 Make the posts. A post resting on a flat rock supports each of the two remaining corners of the deck. Make the posts one at a time. First, choose your flat rock. Next, hammer out a rock-sized depression under one corner of the deck. Tamp the rock into the depression. Hold the post in place and mark it at the top and where it crosses the bottom of the joist. Saw off the top, then saw a ledger the length from the bottom of the joist down to the rock. Screw the two pieces of wood together as shown at center right, creating a rabbet. Plant the post on the rock and tuck the rim joist into the rabbet. Screw the joists to the post, as shown in the photo at far right. Make and fit the last post in the same way.

10 Deck the deck. Arrange the plywood pieces on the deck frame and fasten them with 2½-inch spiral deck nails, spaced 8 inches apart. Paint the deck, or leave it to weather naturally.

Pitch the deck. Bring the low side of the deck to within an inch of level and block it up or clamp it to temporary props.

Make the posts. Plant a flat rock under the corner of the deck and set a post on it (top left). Mark the height of the joist on the post and trim it to length (top right). Nail the ledger to the post (left), then screw the post to the joists (right).

Deck the deck. Arrange the plywood decking and nail it to the frame.

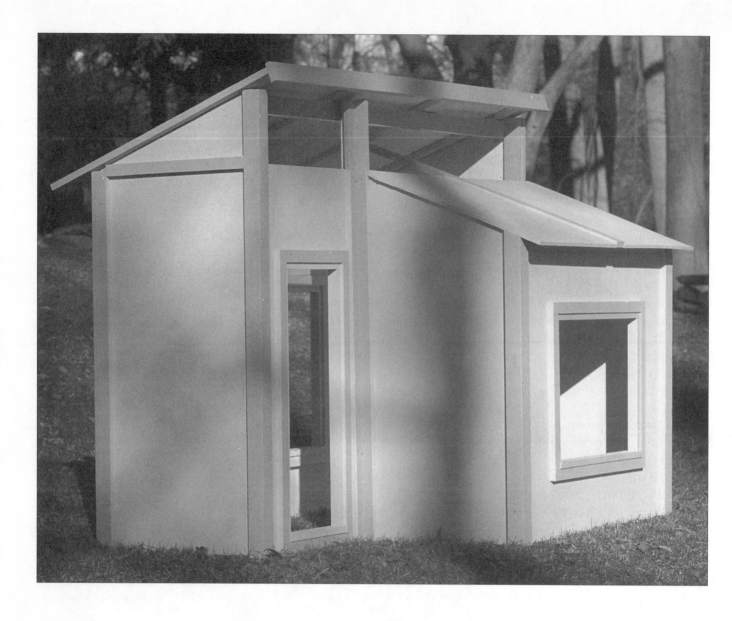

PLAY HOUSE

A castle, a ship, a fort, a place to exercise the young imagination

Little children love a play house. It can be a castle or a hideaway, a fort or a ship. They'll climb on it and inside it, they'll hide behind it and fill it with toys, and given a chance they'll keel over for a nap inside. A robust play house is both an escape from the adult-scale world and a gateway for the young imagination. In England, a substantial play house with door and window openings is called a Wendy house in homage to the Peter Pan story.

This play house has a doorway, a clerestory roof, and as many windows as you like.

There are four important design considerations: size, strength, access, and deconstruction.

The play house should be big enough to accommodate children up to the age of 8 or 9. After that, they lose interest in make-believe play. Most manufactured play houses are too small. They're fine for very young children, but the 6-year-olds and 8-year-olds find they can no longer stand up inside.

The three-piece corner system shown in this project makes a very strong connection. Two of the pieces are permanently glued and screwed to one of the plywood panels, with the third piece glued and screwed to the other panel. You lock each corner with screws but no glue, which allows you to take the joint apart and assemble it again. You could design an equivalent joint with bolts and nuts, but you would have a tough time aligning the holes when reassembling. Screws avoid this difficulty.

Adults should be able to reach inside the play house, even if they can't easily wriggle through the doorway. The adult-sized opening is the front window. Depending on the age and general rowdiness of your children, you could decide to make this opening even larger than the one shown, so you can crawl right in after the scamps. There is a second window in the back wall, and naturally you can make additional openings in the other walls of the play house.

Unless you plan to build the play house on the little deck (page 69) or on a semi-permanent foundation in the back-yard, it's helpful to be able to take it apart and move it or store it. Taking it apart requires removing quite a few screws, and it will consume several hours, but it is possible to do. You may want the play house to be outside for the summer, then relocated to the family room for the winter. And ultimately, you may want to bundle it up and pass it along to another young family, sell it, or squirrel it away for your grandchildren.

BUILDING THE PLAY HOUSE

1 Start with the plywood. Home centers sell plywood cut into 48-inch squares and 24-inch by 48-inch rectangles, for virtually no price premium over full sheets. These pieces are much easier to move and manage than the four 4×8 sheets you would otherwise need. This house requires three 4×4 wall panels and nine 2×4 panels, four for the walls and five for the roof. When you get the plywood into the workshop, begin by mocking up the walls of the play house, as shown in the photo below.

Standing the wall panels in position will orient you. One of the three 4×4 panels forms the wide end, one forms the front, and one forms the wide section of the long back wall. The four 2×4 panels become the narrow end, the door panel, the return wall, and the narrow section of the back wall.

2 Saw the roof line. The slope of the roof comes from sawing triangles of plywood off the return wall and the wide end wall. In Steps 13 and 14, these triangles will be reattached to the narrow end wall and to the back of the wide end wall, creating the clerestory. Start with the 24-inch return wall. Lay out the diagonal cut by measuring 9 inches down from one corner of the sheet, as shown in the top photo on page 77. Cut the wood with the handsaw, jigsaw

Start with the plywood. Lean the plywood panels in position in a corner of the workshop to see how the play house will go together.

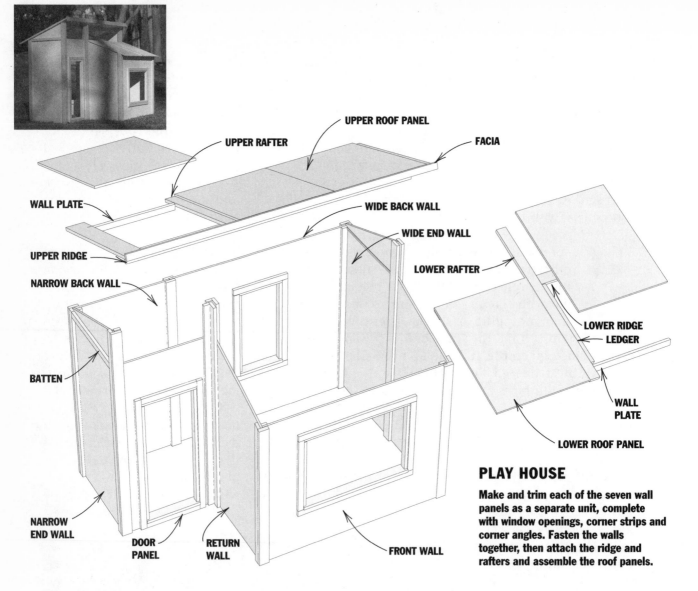

UPPER ROOF PANEL

UPPER RAFTER

FACIA

WALL PLATE

WIDE BACK WALL

WIDE END WALL

UPPER RIDGE

LOWER RAFTER

NARROW BACK WALL

LOWER RIDGE

LEDGER

BATTEN

WALL PLATE

NARROW END WALL

DOOR PANEL

RETURN WALL

FRONT WALL

LOWER ROOF PANEL

PLAY HOUSE

Make and trim each of the seven wall panels as a separate unit, complete with window openings, corner strips and corner angles. Fasten the walls together, then attach the ridge and rafters and assemble the roof panels.

YOUR INVESTMENT

<u>Time:</u> Two weekends
<u>Money:</u> $150

SHOPPING LIST

4 sheets $\frac{1}{2} \times 48 \times 96$ CDX plywood
144 feet 1×2 pine
64 feet 1×3 pine
16 feet 1×5 pine
#6 × 1-inch galvanized screws
#6 × $1\frac{1}{4}$-inch galvanized screws
#6 × $1\frac{5}{8}$-inch galvanized screws
#6 × 2-inch galvanized screws
$2\frac{1}{2}$-inch galvanized siding nails

PROJECT SPECS

The play house measures 77 inches long and 59 inches wide at the eaves, and is 60 inches high at the ridge.

CUTTING LIST

PART	QTY.	DIMENSIONS	NOTES
Wide wall panel	3	$\frac{1}{2} \times 48 \times 48$	CDX plywood
Narrow wall panel	4	$\frac{1}{2} \times 24 \times 48$	CDX plywood
Narrow corner strip	4	$\frac{3}{4} \times 1\frac{1}{2} \times 40$	
Narrow corner strip	4	$\frac{3}{4} \times 1\frac{1}{2} \times 48$	
Narrow corner strip	4	$\frac{3}{4} \times 1\frac{1}{2} \times 57$	
Wide corner strip	2	$\frac{3}{4} \times 2\frac{1}{2} \times 40$	
Wide corner strip	4	$\frac{3}{4} \times 2\frac{1}{2} \times 48$	
Wide corner strip	3	$\frac{3}{4} \times 2\frac{1}{2} \times 57$	
Ridge pole	2	$\frac{3}{4} \times 2\frac{1}{2} \times 57$	
Trim		$\frac{3}{4} \times 1\frac{1}{2} \times 72$ feet	Cut to fit
Sill		$\frac{3}{4} \times 2\frac{1}{2} \times 54$	Cut to fit
Batten	2	$\frac{3}{4} \times 1\frac{1}{2} \times 21$	
Upper ridge	1	$\frac{3}{4} \times 2\frac{1}{2} \times 72$	
Lower ridge	1	$\frac{3}{4} \times 2\frac{1}{2} \times 48$	
Wall plate		$\frac{3}{4} \times 1\frac{1}{2} \times 96$	Cut to fit
Upper rafter	4	$\frac{3}{4} \times 4\frac{1}{2} \times 36$	
Lower rafter	1	$\frac{3}{4} \times 2\frac{1}{2} \times 42$	
Ledger	2	$\frac{3}{4} \times 2\frac{1}{2} \times 22$	Cut to fit
Lower roof panel	2	$\frac{1}{2} \times 24 \times 28\frac{1}{4}$	CDX plywood
Upper roof panel	3	$\frac{1}{2} \times 24 \times 36$	CDX plywood
Fascia	1	$\frac{3}{4} \times 1\frac{1}{2} \times 78$	Trim to fit

or portable circular saw. Now use the offcut to lay out the same cut on one side of the 48-inch panel at the other end of the play house. Finally, saw a 9-inch strip off the top edge of the front wall. The results of this trimming are shown in the photo at center right.

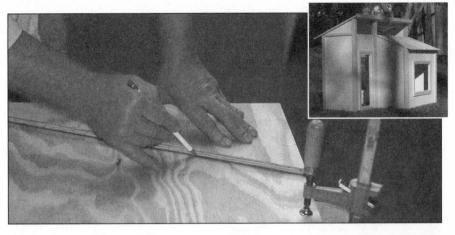

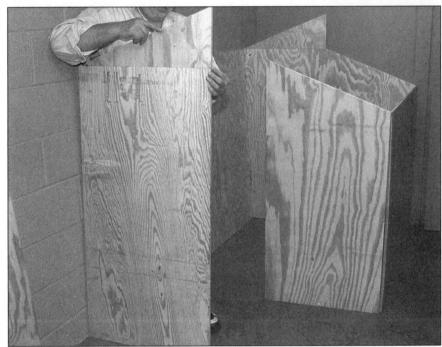

3 **Make the trim, casings and sills.** The trim, casing and sill pieces must be cut to fit the openings you decide to saw in the walls of the play house. The play house as shown has a door and two windows, plus the clerestory openings along the roof. The bill of materials includes enough material to trim and case these openings. If you make more openings, you will need more 1×2 and 1×3 lumber.

4 **Make the corner angles.** Each corner joint needs a right-angle made up of a wide corner strip and a narrow one, glued and screwed together as shown in the photo at bottom right. Roll glue on the edge of the narrow strip and plant the wide strip on it, using a scrap of the 1×2 wood for support. Drill clearance holes and join the two pieces of wood with four of the 2-inch screws. Sand the sharp edges off the wood. Make three 57-inch corner angles, two 48-inch ones, and two 40-inch ones.

Saw the roof line. Measure 9 inches down from the front corner of the return wall and saw off the triangle (top). Trace the triangle onto the wide end wall and saw it off as well. Reattaching the plywood triangles to the two end walls creates the clerestory windows (above).

5 **Make the door panel.** The door panel goes directly under the ridge of the house. It needs a 57-inch corner angle on one edge, and a 57-inch corner strip on the other edge. These pieces extend above the top of the panel and act as ridge poles to support the ridge itself. The

Make the corner angles. Each corner angle consists of a wide corner strip and a narrow one (right). Make up all the corner angles at once.

Make the door panel. Roll glue on the corner strip and fit it flush with the edge of the plywood. Drill and countersink clearance holes, then drive 1-inch screws into the corner strip.

DOOR PANEL

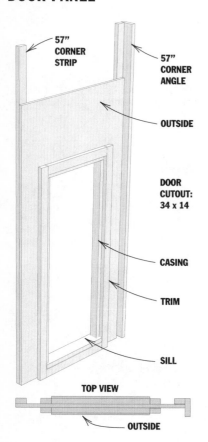

57"
CORNER
STRIP

57"
CORNER
ANGLE

OUTSIDE

DOOR
CUTOUT:
34 x 14

CASING

TRIM

SILL

TOP VIEW

OUTSIDE

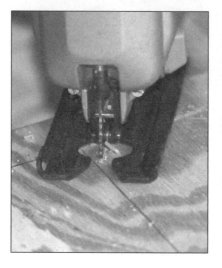

Make the door opening. Brace the toe of the jigsaw on the plywood and firmly lower the reciprocating blade into the wood (above). Saw straight into the corner (left), then back up and saw a curve around the corner (below left). Finally, square up by reversing the saw in the kerf and sawing back into the corner (below right).

panel has an inside and an outside, and therefore a right and a left edge, as shown in the drawing above. Glue and screw the corner angle and the corner strip to the door panel. The wide side of the corner angle lies on the edge of the plywood, with the $1\frac{1}{2}$-inch piece flat on the face. When you see how each piece of wood goes, make a layout line, then drill and countersink clearance holes through the plywood. Roll glue on the inside of the corner angle or corner strip, fit it in place, and drive 1-inch screws to hold it, as shown in the photo at top left.

6 **Make the door opening.** The door opening measures 34 inches high and 14 inches wide. It's centered on the door panel, 1½ inches up from the bottom edge. Lay out and saw the door opening. You can drill a hole to start the jigsaw, or you can ease it into the cut as shown in the top photo on the facing page. To make square corners, saw straight into the corner, back up and turn the corner on a curved path, then saw back into the corner. This maneuver is shown in the bottom three photos on the facing page.

7 **Trim the door opening.** The door trim covers the rough edges of the plywood and also stiffens the panel. It's attached to the face of the plywood by a cut-and-fit process. Begin by trimming the long sides of the opening with pieces that extend from the bottom edge of the panel to 1½ inches beyond the opening at the top. Use scraps of the trim material to gauge the overlap, then make four identical trim pieces. Glue and screw them alongside the door open-

ing, on both sides of the plywood, using the longest screws you can fit. The top and bottom trim fits between the attached pieces of side trim, so mark and cut each of the four pieces to length, then glue and screw them in place, as shown in the photos above and at right.

8 **Case the door opening.** The casing fits inside the door opening, covering the edge of the plywood. It consists of a sill made of 1×3, with a header and side casings made of narrower 1×2 material, same as the trim. The casing is glued and nailed in place with the 2½-inch siding nails. Begin by measuring, cutting and attaching the sill and header, as shown at right. Then complete the opening by fitting the two side casings. Center them on the thickness of the trim pieces. This completes the door panel.

9 **Make the front wall.** The front of the play house is the panel that was trimmed down to 39 inches in Step 2. It's got a narrow corner strip at either side,

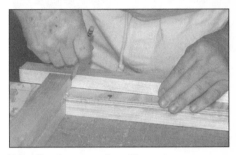

Trim the door opening. Glue, clamp and screw 1×2 trim flush with the edges of the opening (above left). Screw the first piece through the plywood, then screw through the second piece into the plywood (top right). Mark and saw the top trim to fit between the side trim (above).

Case the door opening. Glue and nail the casing inside the opening, covering the plywood edge.

WIDE BACK WALL

TOP VIEW

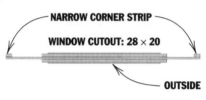

WINDOW CUTOUT: 24 x 12

48" WIDE CORNER STRIP

48" NARROW CORNER STRIP

OUTSIDE

Make the door return. Glue and screw the corner angles to the door return, then saw the short one to match the slope of the roof.

Make the front wall. The window in the front wall provides adult access to the play house, so make it big enough. Trim it, case it and make a wide sill out of 1×3 lumber.

FRONT WALL

TOP VIEW

NARROW CORNER STRIP

WINDOW CUTOUT: 28 × 20

OUTSIDE

NARROW BACK WALL

TOP VIEW

48" NARROW CORNER STRIP

OUTSIDE

48" WIDE CORNER STRIP

RETURN WALL

TOP VIEW

40" CORNER ANGLE

OUTSIDE

57" CORNER ANGLE

and a centered 20-inch by 28-inch window opening. Glue and screw the corner strips to the back face of the plywood, flush with the edges of the sheet. Saw the window opening the same

way you made the door opening in Step 6. Trim and case the window opening the same way you finished the door panel in Steps 7 and 8. Sand the sharp corners off the 1×3 sill.

10 **Make the wide back wall.** The wide back wall has a tall and narrow window opening, which is sawn, trimmed and cased the same as the door opening and the window in the front wall. The wide back wall has a narrow corner strip at one edge, and a wide corner strip at the other edge. The wide corner strip, which makes the connection with the narrow back wall, extends off the plywood by half its width. Glue and screw both corner strips to the inside face of the wide back wall.

11 **Make the narrow back wall.** The narrow back wall is an untrimmed piece of 24-inch × 48-inch plywood. It has a narrow corner strip glued and screwed along one long edge, with a wide corner strip along the other. The wide corner strip goes on the opposite face of the plywood from the narrow corner strip, so it can complete the connection with the wide back wall.

12 **Make the return wall.** The return wall has a 40-inch corner angle attached to its short edge, and a 57-inch corner angle attached to its long edge. Orient the corner strips as shown in the drawing at left. Then trim the 40-inch corner angle to follow the sloped edge of the plywood, as shown in the bottom left photo.

13 **Make the narrow end wall.** The narrow end wall has a 57-inch corner angle along one long edge, with a 48-inch corner angle on the other. The 57-inch corner angle becomes the ridge pole at one end the play house. The narrow end wall has to be extended

by the plywood triangle sawn off the return wall in Step 2. Glue and screw the corner angles to the wall, then fit the plywood triangle, as shown in the photo at right. Attach the triangle with a 1×2 batten, glued and screwed.

14 **Make the wide end wall.** The wide end wall has two ridge posts glued and screwed to its center, one on each face of the plywood, as shown in the photo below. These 57-inch pieces of 1×3 are the same size as the wide corner strips. The wide end wall has a corner angle attached at each edge, as shown in the drawing at right. Trim the 40-inch corner angle to follow the slope sawn into the plywood. Finally, join the plywood triangle sawn from one part of the wide end wall to the other part of the same wall, as shown in the bottom right photo. Screw the plywood to a glued batten, same as in Step 13.

Make the narrow end wall. Glue and screw the two corner angles to the narrow end wall, then fit the plywood triangle atop the wall. Use a straight edge to align it with the corner angle, then attach it to the wall with a 1×2 batten.

NARROW END WALL

TOP VIEW   48" CORNER ANGLE

57" CORNER ANGLE   OUTSIDE

WIDE END WALL

TOP VIEW   48" CORNER ANGLE

40" CORNER ANGLE   OUTSIDE

BATTEN

RIDGE POLE

Make the wide end wall. Attach two ridge poles to the center of the end wall, one on either face of the plywood (left). Slide the plywood triangle into the slot between the ridge poles, align it, and attach it with a 1×2 batten (above).

Assemble the walls. Hold the walls in place with clamps, then screw the corners together (left).

Raise the upper ridge. Clamp the upper ridge to the ridge poles and screw it in place (above).

Make the lower ridge. Fit the lower ridge against the ridge poles and screw into it through the plywood walls.

Make the wall plates. Fit the 1×2 wall plates between the corner angles on the front and back walls. Screw them to the plywood from the inside.

15 **Assemble the walls.** Fit the walls together as shown in the top left photo, and anchor them with screws through each corner angle. You'll probably need a helper to push each joint tight as you drive the 1¼-inch screws. If you are building the play house in your workshop, drive no more than two or three screws through each corner angle, so you can disassemble it in order to move the play house to its final location.

16 **Raise the upper ridge.** The upper ridge is a 6-foot 1×3 that spans the three ridge poles. Clamp it to the back side of the ridge poles, and fasten it with two or three of the 1⅝-inch screws at each intersection.

17 **Make the lower ridge.** The lower ridge is a 4-foot 1×3 that bridges the sloping eaves of the lower roof. Fit it in place as shown in the lower left photo, and screw into the lower ridge

through the plywood panels.

18 **Make the wall plates.** The wall plates stiffen the plywood walls and create attachment points for the lower roof. They are lengths of 1×2 screwed to the outside face of the front and back walls, as shown in the photo above.

19 **Fit the upper rafters.** There are four upper rafters, made of 1×5 wood and installed face-up instead of edge-up. Wood of this width both stiffens the roof and allows making the roof of 24-inch plywood panels. The upper rafters are 36 inches long, with a 5-inch overhang at either end, as shown in the bottom photo at right. Attach each rafter to the wall plate and the ridge with two 2-inch screws at each joint.

20 Make the lower rafter and ledgers. The lower rafter is 42 inches long. Its top end touches the upper rafter, as shown in the photo at top right. Screw it to the wall plate and to the lower ridge, then drive a couple of screws into it through the upper rafter. The ledgers, lengths of 1×3 screwed to the underside of the lower rafter, create a rabbet that will support the roof plywood. Trim them to fit in between the lower ridge and the front wall, and screw them to the rafters.

21 Fit the lower roof. Drop the two lower roof panels onto the ledgers. They'll rest on the top edges of the plywood walls, as shown in the center photos. You'll have to notch one corner of the roof to fit around the center ridge pole.

22 Fit the upper roof. Center the three upper roof panels on the rafters and screw them in place. Use the 1-inch screws. Drive six screws into each long edge, as shown at right.

23 Attach the fascia. The fascia tidies the front edge of the roof. Screw it to the ends of the rafters with a couple of 2-inch screws in each rafter. Trim it to length after it's in place.

24 Finish the play house. You may need to disassemble the play house to move it to its final location, but you'll be able to do so because the assembly joints were all made without glue. Reassemble the house where it will rest, with five or six screws at each corner angle. To make a rudimentary foundation, set a row of bricks under the walls. Protect the playhouse from the weather by painting or staining the wood. We used a second color to pick out the trim pieces and corner angles, as shown in the photo on page 74.

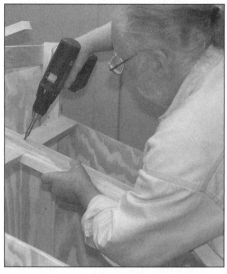

Make the lower rafter and ledgers. Screw the lower rafter to the lower ridge, and to the front wall plate. Attach the ledgers to its underside.

Fit the lower roof. Butt the lower roof panels to the lower rafter (left). Lay out and saw a notch so the left-hand panel fits around the ridge pole (right).

Fit the upper roof. Drop the upper roof onto the rafters. Center the panels and screw them in place.

LOG BENCH

Here's a quick seat made with two rounds and a plank

The log bench is among the simplest of landscape projects, provided you've got a couple of short logs to work with. It's just a pair of round logs with a pair of planks nailed on top. The big decision is where to put the bench, because once you spike the seat planks onto the logs, it won't be easy to move.

The logs in the photos are about 17 inches long and 13 inches in diameter. They came from land clearing. If you have firewood delivered, you should be able to ask for a couple of unsplit rounds, stove length.

Any diameter over 12 inches will make a good bench. Length variations are no problem. The bench will be fine down to about 12 inches high. If the logs are too long and you don't have a chainsaw, you can always dig them a couple of inches into the ground.

As an alternative to the bench shown in the photos, you can lay the logs on their sides, like the wheels of Fred Flintstone's car. You have to choose logs of equal diameter. Drive three spikes through each plank, in a triangular pattern.

BUILDING THE BENCH

1 Prepare the wood. For the seat, select clean, knot-free construction lumber; Douglas fir is best. Avoid pitch pockets, which will ooze sticky pitch until the end of time. Cut your seat material into two planks of equal length. Select or saw logs whose ends are flat and parallel.

2 Spike the seat onto the logs. Drive one or two of the 6-inch galvanized spiral-shank spikes into each end of each plank, as shown in the photo at right.

Spike the seat onto the logs. Set the first seat plank in place and nail through it into the end of the round log. Spike the second seat plank in the same way.

LOG BENCH

Spike the 2×8 seat planks onto the ends of the round logs. As an alternative, spike the planks onto the sides of the logs.

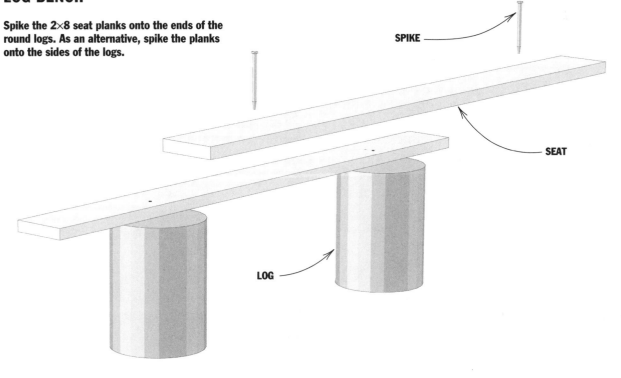

SPIKE

SEAT

LOG

PROJECT SPECS
The slab bench is 18 inches high, 15 inches wide and 7 feet long.

CUTTING LIST

PART	QTY.	DIMENSIONS	NOTES
Log	2	$13 \times 13 \times 17$	
Seat	2	$1\frac{1}{2} \times 7\frac{1}{2} \times 84$	2×8

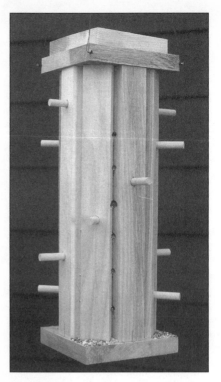

OCTAGONAL BIRD FEEDER

Standard lumber generates interesting shape

The octagonal bird feeder is a symmetrical column that hangs from a single string. It attracts flocks of small birds. The birds alight on the little perches, and peck their meal from the holes drilled into the sides of the octagon.

You can make the octagonal feeder without measuring angles or doing any mathematical calculation. The geometry relies on standard lumber sizes. It's easy to get it to come out right.

BUILDING THE BIRD FEEDER

1 Cut the wood. Begin the project by cutting the top and bottom squares, and the eight side pieces. Make sure that all the side pieces are the same length.

2 Lay out the top and bottom. Although the octagon arises naturally from stock lumber sizes, you do need to make layout lines. First, connect the corners of the square bottom end. This locates its center. Next, draw square lines through the center, as shown in the top left photo on the facing page. Finally, draw lines around the perimeter of the bottom end, ⅛ inch in from the edges of the wood. Lay out the top end the same way.

3 Make the square. Make the octagon in two stages, first by attaching the four sides of a square to the bottom end, then by filling in with the four diagonal pieces. Mark a center line on the end of four of the side pieces. Stand the first piece on one of the centered layout lines, along the ⅛-inch mark. When you see where it goes, start a 2-

YOUR INVESTMENT
<u>Time:</u> One evening
<u>Money:</u> $5

SHOPPING LIST
10 feet 1×2 pine
1 foot 1×5 pine
1 foot 1×6 pine
4 feet ⅜ dowel
2-inch galvanized siding nails

PROJECT SPECS
The octagonal bird feeder is 16 inches high and 5½ inches square.

CUTTING LIST

PART	QTY.	DIMENSIONS	NOTES
End	2	¾ × 5½ × 5½	1×6 pine
Side	8	¾ × 1½ × 14	1×2 pine
Cap	1	¾ × 4½ × 4½	1×5 pine
Perch	16	3 × ⅜ dia.	Dowel

OCTAGONAL BIRD FEEDER

Make the octagon by nailing the side pieces to the bottom end. Drill the top, then nail it onto the side pieces. Attach the plug to the cap. Drill holes for the perches and for the feed to emerge.

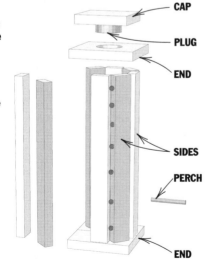

Lay out the top and bottom. Draw center lines and diagonal lines on the wood, then make layout lines 1/8 inch in from the edges (left). Centering the sides on these marks creates the octagon (right).

Make the square. Nail four of the side pieces to the bottom end, to make a square. Brace the wood on the wall.

Attach the top end. Nail the top onto the free ends of the sides. Reach through the hole to align the wood.

Make the cap. Nail the holesaw plug to the cap. Clench the nails on the top side of the cap.

Drill the seed holes. Drill holes in the valley between the side pieces so the birds can peck at the seed.

inch siding nail through the bottom and drive it into the end of the side piece. Anchor it with two more siding nails. Then attach the other three sides of the square in the same way, as shown in the top right photo.

4 Make the octagon. The remaining four side pieces will fill in the sides of the octagon. You might have to sand the corners off the wood to get a tight fit. Nail into each side through the bottom end, as in the previous step.

5 Drill the top end. The top end of the feeder has a large hole, through which you can add birdseed. Drill the hole with a 2-inch or 2 1/4-inch holesaw. Keep the circular plug of waste

for making the cap in Step 7.

6 Attach the top end. Nail the top piece onto the free ends of the side pieces. You'll be able to reach in through the drilled hole to position each piece on the layout lines. Drive one centered nail into the end of each side piece. This leaves you some wiggle room to adjust the pieces as you drive the remaining two nails into each one. Use the 2-inch siding nails, same as for the bottom end.

7 Make the cap. The cap is a square of 1×5 wood with the holesaw plug attached to it. Attach the plug with two of the siding nails, clenched (that s, bent over) on the top side.

8 Make the perches. The little birds that will frequent this feeder like to park on perches, which you can make from 2-inch lengths of 3/8-inch dowel set into the center of the side pieces.

9 Drill the seed holes. Once you've located the perches, drill a couple of feed holes for each. Drill the 1/4-inch holes into the corners of the octagon.

10 Hang the feeder. Suspend the feeder from a cord. Tap a cord-anchoring nail into each corner of the top and bring the four short cords together to a single cord about a foot above the feeder. Loop the cord over a branch or through an eye screwed into an eave, so you can lower the feeder to refill it.

WOODEN SWING

Fly safely through the air on this sturdy structure

Bolt the braces to the posts. Clamp the braces to the posts and drill through holes for the four ⁵⁄₁₆-inch bolts

(left). The 1½-inch overhang at the lower left of the photo will be the bottom of the post. Put a washer under

the head, tap a bolt into the hole and use a socket wrench to tighten a nut against a second washer (right).

A wooden swing brings on sweet nostalgia for childhood in a way that no metal swing-set ever could. A wooden swing speaks of small towns and simpler times, and of coming as close to flying through the air as ordinary mortals can.

Because the swinger does almost fly, it's critically important that the swing not fail. While one could calculate the stresses and engineer it with precision, the practical answer is to overbuild it. A side benefit of overbuilding is, you get a lot of visual interest from the various pieces of wood.

The wooden swing shown here is a 2×4 construction, held together by sturdy bolts and lag screws. The posts have a T-shaped cross section, which makes them enormously stiff. The posts are braced with 2×4 triangles. This is a simple way of achieving incredible strength. You can apply this method to other structural problems around the homestead. For example, shorter posts and a wider crossbeam would make an excellent hoist for lifting

engines out of cars, or for moving machinery into a loft.

Lag screws connect 2×4 parts the same way wood screws connect 1× parts. There has to be a clearance hole the full diameter of the lag screw completely through one piece, with a pilot hole no larger than the root diameter of the screw thread into the other piece. Otherwise, the screw cannot draw the two pieces tightly together. Since this project uses ⁵⁄₁₆-inch lag screws, all the clearance holes will be ⁵⁄₁₆ inch. Drill the pilot holes with a ³⁄₁₆- or ¼-inch bit, for half the length of the thread, and let the lag screw make its own hole the rest of the way. The screws will be a tight fit in their clearance holes, so tap them through with a hammer.

All the bolts and lag screws should be galvanized, to resist rust. However, when you shop for hardware you may find not all sizes available in the galvanized section. In that case, it's better to use regular zinc-plated hardware of the correct size, instead of oversized or undersized galvanized hardware.

BUILDING THE SWING

1 Cut all the wood. It's not easy to manage 10-foot and 12-foot 2×4s, so it's best to set up for crosscutting and saw all the material to length at one time. The mitered braces all can be trimmed out of the lengths given in the cutting list.

2 Bolt the braces to the posts. Four bolts hold each post and brace together, creating a T-shaped cross section. This makes an extraordinarily strong and stiff structure. Lay the post flat on the worktable and center the brace on it. Make the two pieces flush at the top end, with an inset of 1½ inches at the bottom, and clamp them together. Lay out and drill holes for four ⁵⁄₁₆-inch bolts, as shown in the photos above. Locate the first two holes 6 inches from either end of the brace. The other two holes will be 30 inches away, and 30 inches apart. Slip a washer onto each bolt, tap it into its hole, slip a second washer and a nut onto the other side, and tighten the nut with a wrench.

WOODEN SWING

Make the swing as five subassemblies: two posts, beam with yokes, and two bases. Begin by bolting the two posts to the post braces. Make the beam and fasten the yokes to it. Make the two base assemblies. Attach the outriggers to the posts. Assemble the swing on level ground.

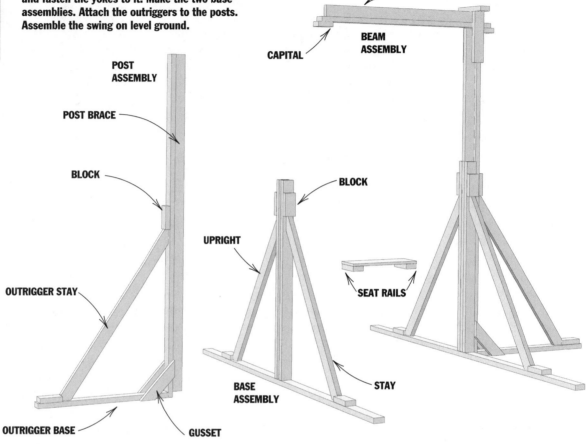

YOKE
TIE
POST RETAINER
BEAM BRACE
CAPITAL
BEAM ASSEMBLY

POST ASSEMBLY
POST BRACE
BLOCK
BLOCK
UPRIGHT
SEAT RAILS
OUTRIGGER STAY
BASE ASSEMBLY
STAY
OUTRIGGER BASE
GUSSET

YOUR INVESTMENT

Time: All weekend
Money: $60 wood, $60 hardware

SHOPPING LIST

15 10-foot 2×4, Douglas fir
17 $^5/_{16}$ × 5 $^1/_2$-inch hex-head bolts with washers and nuts (posts and beam)
2 $^1/_2$ × 8-inch eye bolts with washers and nuts (chain)
4 $^5/_{16}$ × 8-inch hex-head bolts with washers and nuts (yoke)
22 $^5/_{16}$ × 5-inch galvanized lag screws
12 $^5/_{16}$ × 3-inch galvanized lag screws
6 12-inch galvanized landscape spikes
16 feet $^3/_8$-inch steel chain
4 $^5/_{16}$ × 5-inch eye bolts
4 $^1/_4$-inch U bolts
2 $^5/_{16}$-inch U bolts

PROJECT SPECS

The wooden swing is 9 feet 2 inches high, 10 feet front to back at the base, and 12 feet wide at the outriggers. The swing space is 4 feet wide.

CUTTING LIST

PART	QTY.	DIMENSIONS	NOTES
Post	2	$1^1/_2 × 3^1/_2 × 103^1/_2$	2×4
Post brace	2	$1^1/_2 × 3^1/_2 × 102$	2×4
Beam	1	$1^1/_2 × 3^1/_2 × 62$	2×4
Beam brace	1	$1^1/_2 × 3^1/_2 × 58$	2×4
Capital	2	$1^1/_2 × 3^1/_2 × 5$	2×4
Tie	2	$1^1/_2 × 3^1/_2 × 13$	2×4
Post retainer	4	$1^1/_2 × 3^1/_2 × 16$	2×4
Stay	4	$1^1/_2 × 3^1/_2 × 60$	2×4; miter
Base	2	$1^1/_2 × 3^1/_2 × 120$	2×4
Upright	4	$1^1/_2 × 3^1/_2 × 60$	2×4
Outrigger stay	2	$1^1/_2 × 3^1/_2 × 60$	2×4; miter
Outrigger base	2	$1^1/_2 × 3^1/_2 × 42$	2×4
Block	12	$1^1/_2 × 3^1/_2 × 7$	2×4
Gusset	4	$1^1/_2 × 3^1/_2 × 16$	2×4; miter 45°
Seat	1	$^3/_4 × 7^1/_2 × 22$	1×8
Seat rail	2	$1^1/_2 × 3^1/_2 × 7$	2×4

Brace the second post in the same way.

3 Make the beam. The beam and beam brace make a T-shaped section, same as the posts, and they are held together in the same way, except with only three bolts instead of four. Two of the bolts fall 8 inches in from either end, with the third bolt on center. Clamp the two parts together, with the beam brace centered from end to end and side to side. Block the beam parts up on scraps of 2×4, for drilling clearance.

4 Install the eye bolts. Two substantial ½-inch eye bolts support the chains and the swing. While you have the beam on the worktable, drill the holes and install the eye bolts. The holes should be 12 inches from either end of the beam brace. To avoid a splintered exit hole, drill through the edge of the brace until the point of the spade bit just emerges through the bottom face of the beam. Then turn the beam over and complete the hole from the other side. Slip a ½-inch washer onto the eye bolt, tap it into the hole, then add a second washer against the nut, as shown in the photos above.

5 Attach the capitals. The capitals locate the beam atop the posts. The post retainers and ties make a yoke which will connect the beam to the posts, in Step 7. While you have the beam on the worktable, lag-screw a capital at each end. The 5-inch capitals overhang the end of the beam by 1 inch. Drill clearance holes for a 3-inch lag screw down through the capital into

Attach the capitals. Clamp the capitals to the ends of the beam and fasten them with lag screws (above).

Install the eye bolts. Drill ½-inch holes through the beam and install the eye bolts. Put a washer under the eye as well as under the nut (left).

Make the yokes. Clamp the two retainers together and drill a ⁵⁄₁₆-inch bolt hole through them both (left). Space the retainers with a 2×4 scrap and lag-screw the tie piece to them (right).

the beam, and for a second 3-inch lag screw up through the beam into the capital.

6 Make the yokes. The yokes are U-shaped assemblies consisting of two post retainers connected by a tie piece. They guarantee the connection between the swing beam and the posts. You have to drill the holes and assemble the pieces in order, or you will have alignment problems. Begin by clamping the two

retainers together face to face, and square a layout line across them, 4¼ inches from one end. Drill a centered ⁵⁄₁₆-inch clearance hole through both pieces. Now unclamp them and set them up on the worktable with a 2×4 spacer, as shown in the photo above. This spacer represents the swing beam, allowing you to locate and two drill clearance holes in the tie. Fasten the tie to the retainers with two of the 5-inch lag screws.

7 Join the yokes and beam. Fit the completed yokes onto the beam as shown in the photo at left. The yokes should embrace the beam and overlap the edge of the capitals by about ¼ inch. Use the clearance hole you already drilled in the retainers as a guide for drilling completely through the edge of the beam. Attach each yoke to the beam with an 8-inch hex-head bolt. This bolt will be too long, but you probably can't find a 7-inch one, so make it tight by packing the bolt head and nut with extra washers.

8 Make the stays. The two base assemblies each consist of two 2×4 triangles which, when lag-screwed to the posts, keep the swing vertical in the front and back direction. When the stays are joined to the base and uprights, they become the long sides or hypotenuses of right-angle triangles. To make a neat joint, the ends of the stays must be mitered at 35 degrees and 55 degrees, as shown in the drawing below. If you have a chop saw, use it to cut these angles. Otherwise, jigsaw one stay, then use it as a pattern to lay out the others. Make the long cut at either end first. The short cut is at 90 degrees to the long cut, so it can be laid out with a square. Make six identical stays: four for the base assembly, and two for the outriggers.

Join the yokes and beam. Extend the holes in the retainers through the beam, and bolt the parts together.

STAY DETAIL

LAY OUT THE ANGLED ENDS OF THE STAYS BY DIRECT MEASUREMENT, OR WITH A PROTRACTOR.

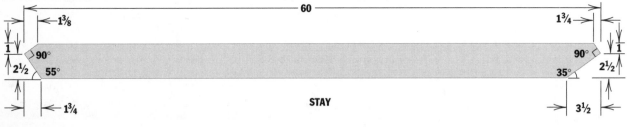

STAY

Make the stays. Jigsaw the angled ends of the first stay (left). Use it as a pattern to make the other five stays (right).

9 **Screw the uprights to the base.** The two base assemblies each consist of a 10-foot base, two uprights and two diagonal stays. Complete one base assembly, then make the other. The two uprights are lag-screwed to the base piece at its center. The uprights ultimately will be bolted to the posts, so they need to be spaced the thickness of the 2×4 post apart, by clamping them to a gauge piece, as shown in the photo at right. Drill $\frac{5}{16}$-inch clearance holes through the base, then change bits and drill $\frac{1}{4}$-inch pilot holes several inches into the end of each upright.

10 **Attach the stays.** Clamp the assembled base and uprights to the worktable, making sure they're at right angles to one another. The stays must now be lag-screwed to the upright and base. Fit the first stay in position, blocked up on scrap so it's centered in the width of the wood. Be sure you get it right way up: the top of the stay should be about 48 inches from the base. Measure $2\frac{1}{4}$ inches down from the top end of the stay and square a line, as shown in the photo at center left. Drill a $\frac{5}{16}$-inch clearance hole through the stay on this line, as shown in the photo at center right. Put the stay back in position, drill a pilot hole, and drive the 5-inch lag screw into the upright. At the base, push the stay toward the upright and clamp a block to anchor it. Then drill a clearance hole through the base, a pilot hole into the upright, and drive a 5-inch lag screw. Join the second stay to the other end of the base in the same way. And now

Screw the uprights to the base. Clamp the two uprights to a 2×4 spacer and lag-screw them in the center of the 10-foot base piece.

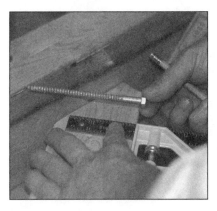

Attach the stays. Square a line across the top of the stay where the lag screw will fit (above). Drill a clearance hole (right) and fasten the stay to the upright. At the bottom end, drill up through the base into the stay (below).

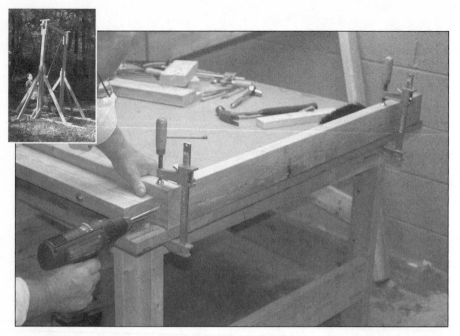

Make the outrigger base. Clamp the post and outrigger base in position, and drill through the post into the end of the base (above). Drive a lag screw (below).

Attach the outrigger stay. Lag-screw the outrigger stay to the base and post.

Reinforce the stays with blocks. Glue and screw a block against each end of all the stays.

that you have completed one base assembly, make the other in exactly the same way.

11 Make the outrigger base. The outrigger stay and outrigger base attach directly to the post, with 5-inch lag screws. Clamp the post to the worktable as shown in the photo above, and

bring the outrigger base up to the bottom of the post. It will be screwed to the bit of post that overhangs the post brace, on the opposite side from the post brace. Clamp the outrigger base in position, square to the post. Drill a $5/16$-inch clearance hole through the post overhang, and a $1/4$-inch pilot hole about 2

inches into the end-grain of the outrigger base. Complete the joint with a 5-inch lag screw.

12 Attach the outrigger stay. The outrigger stay completes the triangle described by the post and outrigger base. Fit it in position the same way you positioned the base stays. Drill clear ance holes and pilot holes, and fasten it to the post and to the outrigger base with a 5-inch lag screw at each end, as shown at left. Attach the other outrigger base and stay to the other post in the same way.

13 Reinforce the stays with blocks. Blocks, glued and screwed at both ends of each diagonal stay, guarantee the integrity of the construction. Spread glue on each block, clamp it tight against the end of the stay, and screw it to the face of the post, upright or base piece with two of the 3-inch wood screws, as shown at left.

14 Drill two clearance holes. When you assemble the swing, you'll find that the head of the lag screw joining the outrigger base to the post has nowhere to go. It needs a shallow clearance hole. Drill a $1\frac{1}{4}$-inch hole $\frac{1}{2}$-inch deep in the center of the edge of the base, as shown in the photo at right. Drill this shallow clearance hole on one side of each base assembly.

15 Make the swing seat. The seat is a 1×8 pine board with two rails screwed cross-grain beneath it. An eye bolt and shackle at each corner connects the seat to the chain. Attach the seat to each rail with four 2-inch screws. Drill $\frac{5}{16}$-inch holes for the eye bolts, $1\frac{1}{2}$ inches in from the edges of the seat and 2 inches in from either end. Put a washer under the eye and also under the nut on each bolt, as shown in the photo at top right. Then cover the exposed thread with a second nut jammed tight against the first one.

Drill two clearance holes. The shallow clearance hole in the center of the base fits over the lag screw in the outrigger.

Make the swing seat. Screw the seat to the rails, then fit an eye bolt at each corner.

Position the posts and beam. Fit the parts together, with the top of the posts trapped between the retainers and tight against the capitals. Tack a spacer across the bottom of the swing and measure the diagonals to check for square.

16 Position the posts and beam. The first step in assembling the swing is to position and connect the posts and the beam. This means finding a large place to work, which can be an empty garage, outdoors on a deck, or on sawhorses in the yard, as shown in the photo below. The posts fit into the yoke, between the retainers. They stop against the capitals. Get them square with a framing square, then measure the distance between the posts at the beam end. Make a piece of scrap

Join the posts to the retainers. Drill clearance holes and lag-screw the retainers to the posts (above). Screw gussets between the posts and outrigger base pieces (right).

Raise the contraption. Stand the swing subassemblies upright and fit them together (left). Clamp each post into its slot in the base, then drill clearance holes and bolt the pieces together (right).

this same length and screw it across the post braces near the other end. This ensures that the posts are parallel. Now measure the diagonals and nudge the parts until they are equal, whereupon the swing is square. Clamp it to the sawhorses.

17 Join the posts to the retainers. Drill two $5/16$-inch clearance holes through each retainer, for two of the 3-inch lag screws. Drive them into the edge of the posts. Before you turn the assembly over to do the other side, screw a gusset at the bot

tom of each post, spanning the edges of the post and of the outrigger base, as shown in the photo below. The gusset makes sure the outrigger never loses its grip on the post. Now enlist a friend to help you turn the assembly over, so you can screw

Level and stake the swing to the ground. Drill and drive a 12-inch landscape spike at tne end of each base piece.

Hang the swing. Three shackles connect the swing seat to each chain (right). Larger shackles join the chain to the eye bolt in the swing beam (below).

the retainers and gussets to the other side of the swing. Don't let the friend escape, because you will need more help in Step 18.

18 **Raise the contraption.** Find level ground and lug the two base assemblies and the posts-and-beam assembly there. Stand the post assembly up vertical. Have your helper hold it up while you slide the base assemblies onto the post braces. You might have to lift each post to slide the base under the brace. Tug the pieces tight together with clamps, as shown in the photos at bottom left. Drill a $^5/_{16}$-inch bolt hole clear through the uprights and brace at the top, center and bottom. Install a $5^1/_2$-inch hex-head bolt in each hole.

19 **Level and stake the swing to the ground.** Go around the base of the swing and see what you can do to bring the ends of each base piece into firm contact with the ground. You may need to dig some earth away, and you may need to install

some wooden wedges. Once everything is as solid as you can make it, drill a $^3/_8$ inch hole through each base piece, near the ends farthest from the posts. Angle these holes toward the posts and drive a 12-inch landscape spike into the ground, as shown in the top left photo.

20 **Hang the swing.** Iron shackles connect the chain to the eye

bolts in the beam and seat. The chains make a short Y about 6 inches above the seat itself, as shown in the photo above. The height of the seat above the ground is entirely up to you. Cut the chain with a chain-cutting tool, or clamp it in a vise and hacksaw it. Tighten all of the screw pins in the shackles. Now the swing is ready for a test flight.

It might be wonderful to have a workshop in which to build and putter. But if you don't have the ideal workspace, you must not let that stop you from making things. No matter where you live, you can find enough space someplace. All you really need is a worktable, some shelves or a cabinet for tools, and some storage for screws, nails, glue, and paint.

Space

Most homeowners set up shop in an unfinished portion of the basement, or in the space alongside or in front of the car. It's difficult to share shop space with other activities because you may need to leave your project until you can get back to it. An 8×8 space is about the minimum—that's the size of a prefab garden shed, or one-sixth of a single-car garage, or an extra room too small for a bedroom. The workspace doesn't have to be any particular shape. An unused storm porch, a few feet wide but running the full length of the house, can be an extraordinarily pleasant place to work, because it's flooded with light.

Another way to get natural light it is to store your tools and

WORKTABLE

The worktable features a knockdown joint based on a dowel and an eye bolt. It's most likely that once you've made the table you won't want to take it apart again, but it's nice to know that you could. You also could use the joint for many of the outdoor projects in this book. It's strong, it can be tightened, and it's not difficult to make.

BUILDING THE TABLE

1. Cut the wood. The table shown is 48 inches on each side, and 29 inches high. You could make one 24 × 48 by shortening half of the rails from 35 inches to 17 inches.

2. Make the legs. Each leg is an angle assembled from a leg piece and a brace piece. Glue and clamp the pieces together, drill four clearance holes, and drive the #8 × 3-inch galvanized screws. Assemble the other three legs in the same way.

3. Lay out the joints. Lay out the slots and the dowel holes, as shown in the drawing. Verify the layout with the eye bolts themselves, as shown in the photo at right.

4. Drill the dowel holes. Drill the holes for the dowels before you saw the slots, otherwise the drill will splinter the wood. Drill about 2½ inches deep.

5. Jigsaw the slots. Saw both sides of the slots, then work the saw back and forth to nibble the ends square.

6. Install the dowels and bolts. Saw a 3-inch length of ¾-inch dowel for each joint. Spread glue on the dowels, set the eye bolt in the slot, and tap the dowel into the hole. Make sure it catches the eye and enters the wood below.

7. Drill holes in the legs. Position the rails against the legs to transfer the location of the slots, as shown in the photo at bottom right. Drill the $^5/_{16}$-inch holes to match the shanks of the eye bolts.

8. Assemble the table. Fit the parts together, slip a washer onto each eye bolt, and tighten the nuts with a socket wrench. Drop the top in place. A top of medium-density fiberboard is heavy enough to stay put.

worktable alongside the car. When you open the garage door to remove the car, leave it open and move your worktable right into the opening. If your only alternative is a windowless cellar, you'll be better off to carry your equipment onto the deck. Don't overlook the spare bedroom, either. You won't make that much noise, and with a good shop vacuum, you can keep the sawdust and debris out of the carpets.

Worktable

For projects like the ones in this book, you need a low assembly table more than you need a regular woodworking bench. Most benches are counter height, 34 to 36 inches, but you'll find it very convenient to work at 28 to 30 inches, or table height, as shown in the project below. To get started, buy a worktable top of 1-inch MDF or two layers of plywood, and drop it across a pair of sawhorses that you make yourself or buy at the home center. The most important thing about the worktable is being able to clear it and sweep it off. This means all your tools and materials need homes of their own.

Lay out the joints. Verify the layout by referring to the actual eye bolts and dowels you plan to use.

Drill holes in the legs. Transfer the hole centers from the slots in the rails.

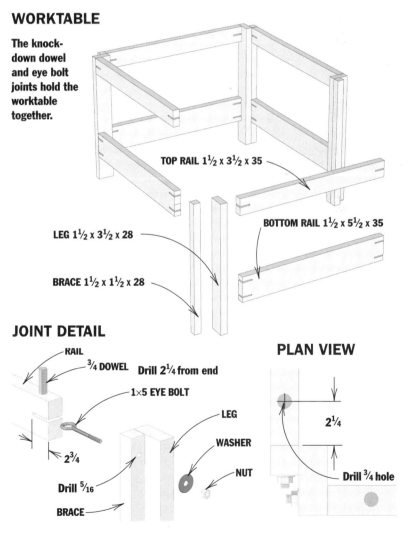

WORKTABLE

The knock-down dowel and eye bolt joints hold the worktable together.

TOP RAIL $1\frac{1}{2}$ x $3\frac{1}{2}$ x 35

BOTTOM RAIL $1\frac{1}{2}$ x $5\frac{1}{2}$ x 35

LEG $1\frac{1}{2}$ x $3\frac{1}{2}$ x 28

BRACE $1\frac{1}{2}$ x $1\frac{1}{2}$ x 28

JOINT DETAIL

RAIL
$\frac{3}{4}$ DOWEL   Drill $2\frac{1}{4}$ from end
1×5 EYE BOLT
LEG
WASHER
NUT
$2\frac{3}{4}$
Drill $\frac{5}{16}$
BRACE

PLAN VIEW

$2\frac{1}{4}$
Drill $\frac{3}{4}$ hole

UTILITY SHELVES

Shelving can be made in almost any size. However, don't make units wider than 30 inches. When you want more width, make two units and stand them side by side. Wide shelves are awkward to move and liable to twist or sag under the weight of motorcycle parts and bowling balls.

To build the unit, make two ladder-like side panels and connect them with the long rails and shelves. Each side panel consists of two uprights joined at the floor by a short rail, then by the ledgers. Ledger construction allows you to make each shelf from two or three narrow pieces of wood. Glue and screw the uprights to the rails, and the ledgers to the uprights. Nail the shelves onto the ledgers with 2-inch siding nails. There's no need to glue.

Tool and material storage

Open shelves work best for tools and materials, such as the ones shown at left. You can glue and screw shelf units together as you need them. Make the shelves 10 inches to 13 inches apart, and make the shelf units 24 inches to 30 inches wide. Any wider than that, and the unit will be awkward to move and liable to sag. It's tempting to make adjustable shelves, but it's rarely worth the trouble. It's more important to gain the rigidity that comes from securely joining every shelf to the ledgers.

To anchor the shelves to a wall, screw a rail between the uprights, directly beneath the top shelf. Then nail through it into a wall stud.

Wood storage

Wood and plywood take a lot of space to store and they are difficult to store correctly. They have to be stored dry and flat. They're heavy and awkward. The pieces you want are always on the bottom of the pile. And you rarely have enough of anything on hand for your next project, so you'll have to go shopping anyway. It's better not to attempt storing a lot of lumber or plywood. You won't be able to avoid accumulating some short ends and extra pieces. Stand them around the walls of the shop and use them freely for general repairs around the house. When you want to start a new project, go to the home center or lumberyard to buy the materials you need.

UTILITY SHELVES

TOP SHELF ¾ x 13 x 28

UPRIGHT ¾ x 2½ x 66

LEDGER ¾ x 1½ x 11

SHELF ¾ x 13 x 26¼

SHORT RAIL ¾ x 4½ x 11

LONG RAIL ¾ x 4½ x 28

All the projects in this book can be made of softwood lumber from the home center or local lumberyard. Most of them use nothing more exotic than ordinary 1× and 2× pine boards. Although a few originally were made with rough-sawn pine from a local sawmill, you can substitute regular lumberyard materials. You could also substitute a durable hardwood such as white oak if you prefer.

There is no need for pressure-treated or chemically preserved lumber. None of the available treatments make environmental sense, and wooden constructions are not particularly vulnerable to water damage, as long as they can drain and dry. Most of the time, when a wooden structure finally does give up to the elements, it's past time for it to go. Let it sink gently into the earth, while you build something new.

Buying enough wood

The cutting lists in this book give the actual size of the pieces of wood you need. If there's a round end or a miter, it will fit within the rectangular dimensions given.

The project shopping lists have been inflated by 15% to 20%. You need to buy that much extra in order to work around knots and other defects, and to give yourself a margin for error. At the end of most of these projects, you'll be left with a box of resinous scrap for starting the barbecue, a stack of short ends, and perhaps an extra board.

How to speak board feet

Lumber sizes are mysterious and the guy at the lumberyard is not about to explain. The first thing to know is, you paid for more wood than you actually got. The reason is, what they sawed out of the log was rough, and what you bought was smooth. In order to make it smooth, they had to shave some wood off the width and the thickness. You're paying not only for the wood you got, but also for what they planed off. When you buy beef it's the other way around, so go figure.

Lumber thickness is measured in quarters of an inch, width is measured in inches, and length is measured in feet. The width and thickness measurements are the rough-sawn size, even if you are buying smooth lumber. The difference between rough and smooth is about $\frac{1}{4}$ inch in thickness, and $\frac{1}{2}$ inch in width. You generally can buy any length you want, as long as you're willing to round up to the next 2-foot increment.

In an attempt to make sense of lumber measure, the marketplace restates thickness measurements in inches. Thus, what the wholesale trade knows as 4/4 lumber (pronounced "four-quarter") will be sold to you as 1× (pronounced "one-by") lumber. It started out about an inch thick, but after drying and smooth-planing, it's about $\frac{3}{4}$ inch thick. This is what you commonly find at the lumberyard and home center. You can also buy a 5/4 board, which started out $1\frac{1}{4}$ inches thick and will be about $1\frac{1}{8}$ inches when planed smooth.

The usual sizes of lumber are 1×2, 1×3, 1×4, 1×5, 1×6, 1×8, 1×10 and 1×12. The actual widths are about a half-inch less, a little wider in narrow boards, but somewhat narrower in wide boards. Most 1×2 lumber comes in at $1\frac{5}{8}$ inches wide, but 1×12 lumber will be closer to $11\frac{1}{4}$ inches.

You don't often find solid wood wider than 12 inches. But wide panels glued up from narrow 4/4 or 5/4 boards are increasingly available. Common widths are $17\frac{1}{2}$ inches and $23\frac{1}{2}$ inches, in 4-foot and 6-foot lengths. While not ideal for outdoor construction, these panels are generally made of sound material and are very useful for indoor projects.

Construction lumber, which starts out 8/4 or two inches thick, is sold as 2× or "two-by", and it actually measures $1\frac{1}{2}$ inches thick. Common sizes are 2×2, 2×4, 2×6 and 2×8.

Home centers and lumberyards sell wood by linear feet, or running feet. It's easy for the customer to understand, but it requires them to maintain a menu of prices covering every width and thickness. If you go to a small sawmill and buy rough-sawn lumber, you'll find yourself in the world of board feet, with a single board-foot price for each species and grade in the yard, regardless of width or thickness.

A board foot is an imaginary piece of wood that's 1 inch thick, 12 inches wide, and 1 foot long. When you buy wood at a sawmill, they convert its actual dimensions to the equivalent number of board feet, then charge you for the board-foot total. If board feet make sense to you, go ahead and check the calculation. If board feet don't make sense to you, don't worry about it. The lumber trade customarily avoids arguments by always rounding calculations in the customer's favor.

Wood species

Most of the 1× lumber you can buy in North America is pine. "Pine," however, can refer to a large number of tree species, which may even include hemlock, spruce, larch, and fir. What all these woods have in common is their origin, from needle-bearing trees, their general white or yellow color, and their relative softness.

Other wood species you'll encounter at the home center include cedar, generally in the form of shingles and shakes, redwood or sequoia, a brown, rot-resistant and expensive softwood, and Douglas fir, North America's preeminent 2× construction timber. Douglas fir is pink in color, and it is heavier and stiffer than pine.

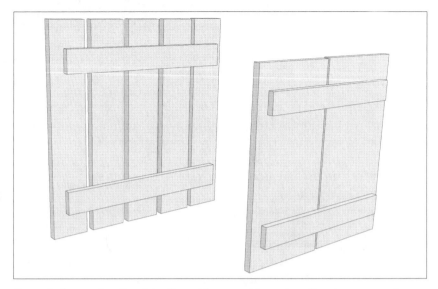

Cross-grain construction in softwood is no problem when the pieces are relatively narrow. Plastic-resin glues, such as ordinary yellow wood glue, have some give. However, a wide cross-grain construction (right) is liable to break apart.

Wood movement

Wood ain't plastic; it comes off living trees, which have a cellular structure. It's the nature of wood cells to respond to moisture: They swell in width and thickness when wet, and they shrink when dry. Wet or dry, they hardly change in length. Harvesting and drying the wood doesn't change its moisture response. When the air gets wet, boards swell. When the air gets dry, boards shrink. Paint or varnish slow down the exchange of moisture between the wood and the air, but nothing stops it.

The problem with wood movement is cross-grain construction, as shown in the photo above. If you glue and screw two pieces of wood in the shape of a cross, the central overlap is cross-grain. Both pieces of wood move in width, but neither changes its length. Too much movement, and the glue gives up.

A piece of wood will be at its smallest indoors in the extreme dryness of wintertime heating. It will be at its largest in muggy summer weather. The amount of wood movement depends on the species as well as on the severity of the moisture cycle. In most softwoods, the maximum potential swing is between ¼ inch and ½ inch per foot of width. If the wood stays outdoors, never experiencing the indoor dryness of winter, the swing is less than half as great.

This is why you can generally ignore wood movement when you build outdoor projects. Movement on the order of $\frac{1}{16}$ inch to ⅛ inch is within the plastic tolerance of softwood and modern glues. And anyway, outdoor woodworking projects are not fine antiques. They are going to change under the onslaught of the elements. Even when a piece of wood does split, if you have followed the construction details given in this book, the project itself is not likely to come apart.

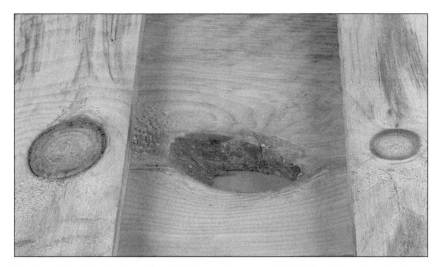

Knots with a black ring of bark (left) are loose and will fall out, leaving a knot-hole (center). Red knots and brown knots (right) are tight. They won't fall out.

All knots point toward the center of the tree. A spike knot (above) may indicate serious weakness.

Knots and defects

Most pine lumber is No. 2 grade, which means it has its share of knots and other defects. You could find clear pine, but you wouldn't like its premium price. Nevertheless, you can get virtually clear wood for your projects by selecting your No. 2 lumber with care, and by managing or eliminating the defects you find in it. For this reason the self-service home center may be a better source than the full-service lumberyard: You can choose your wood yourself. On the other hand, the boards might be so picked over that you're better off with what rises off the pile at the lumberyard.

Always take your cutting list and your tape measure when you go to buy wood. Try to have the major pieces of your project in mind, so you can select wood specifically for them.

Begin by looking at both surfaces of each board. If it runs out to bark at one edge, or it has gross splits or sawmill dings, reject it. Next, look at the knots. Each knot represents a branch, and all softwood branches origi-

Defects such as waney, or bark covered, edges and splits should be sawn out of the wood. The split in the top board was caused by a spike knot.

nate in the center, or pith, of the tree. There are two kinds of knots, black or loose knots, and red or tight knots, as shown in the photo at top left.

Black knots usually include a ring of bark, indicating that after the branch died, the tree trunk grew around it. They'll become loose and fall out, leaving a knot-hole. Red knots, which have no ring of bark, represent living branches. They may crack but they won't fall out. You can work with red knots but you should avoid black knots, or if you can't

avoid them, knock them out. Otherwise, the saw may throw the loose knot into your face.

In pine, the branches tend to grow in whorls, so there may be rows of knots separated by clear wood. You may be able to saw totally clear wood in between rows of knots. However, if you look closely you'll see that the wood's figure is distorted for several inches around the knot itself. While you can incorporate knots and distorted grain in the center of a board, you can't nail it or cut joints in it.

The end grain tells where the board grew in the tree and how it may behave. The 2×4 at left is quartersawn, stable in size and not likely to distort. The flatsawn board next to it is liable to cup. In the middle, tight annual rings indicate strong, slow-grown wood (center left) while wide rings indicate weaker, fast-grown wood (center right). At right, the center 2×4 contains the unstable pith of the tree and you can see that it is not flat. It may also twist. The bottom 2×4, sawn just off the pith, will be more stable, while the top one is rift-sawn and the most stable among this trio. But the most desirable piece of wood in the photo is the quartersawn 2×4 at left.

Now look at the end of the boards. You'll see curved lines, each one representing a year of growth, as shown in the photo above. The spacing of the annual rings tells you how fast the tree grew, and their curvature tells you where the board was inside the tree trunk, which indicates how the wood will behave. Fast-grown softwood, with fewer than five rings to the inch, is weaker than slow-grown softwood, though it's strong enough for most purposes. Boards cut just off the center of the tree are more likely to cup than boards cut from dead center or from farther out. The very center of the tree, called the pith, is unstable wood and should be sawn out of 1× boards and discarded.

Other common defects include pitch pockets, blue or brown stain, and insect holes. When a board oozes gooey pitch, it will continue to do so forever, no matter how many coats of finish you put on it. You can use the board in some unobtrusive place, but not for the seat of a bench. Blue stain and brown stain, caused by fungi and microbes, are harmless discolorations. They don't affect the strength of the wood or its ability to take a finish. Insect holes are no problem, because the culprits will have been killed by the lumber-drying process.

Plywood

There's all kinds of plywood at the home center, but what you want for outdoor projects is exterior grade with one reasonably good face. Buy plywood according to the three-letter grade stamped on each sheet. The most common grade is CDX, where the C and the D refer to the quality of the surfaces, and the X means waterproof glue for exterior use. For projects like the ones in this book, where you're likely to get up close to the finished piece, BDX plywood is generally better than CDX.

Although plywood is stable in length and width, it's rarely flat. This doesn't matter because in most applications you'll nail it onto a structure.

Another useful plywood-type of material is T1-11 siding. Despite its X rating, most plywood ends up covered by other materials. T1-11 is a plywood that's designed to be on show, and also to shed whatever the weather throws at it. It's cheap, strong and durable—an excellent all-around material for utility and garden projects.

You can't make anything nice without measuring tools. You'll use them all the time, every time you cut and connect two pieces of wood. Measuring tools for woodworking commonly measure distance and angles. While you might have a protractor for measuring angles, most of the time the angle of interest is 90 degrees, or square. Distance, of course, is a totally variable number, but a corner or intersection is either 90 degrees or it isn't.

Straightedges and squares are also invaluable for aligning parts. The parts line up or they don't, and if they're off, they have to be wiggled and shoved until they finally do align.

Combination square

The combination square combines a 12-inch straightedge with a 90-degree sliding stock. Thus it can measure both distance and squareness. It's especially useful as a gauge for locating two parts relative to one another, as shown in the photos at top. The sliding stock also has a 45-degree fence for miters.

Speed square

The plastic speed square is a recent addition to the measuring arsenal. Most builders use it instead of the larger and more cumbersome rafter square. The speed square is extremely useful for squaring and aligning parts, as shown in the photos at right.

Tape measure

Splurge for a 25-foot metal tape with a 1-inch blade. Notice that the little metal hook that keeps the blade from disappearing into the case isn't a tight fit. It wiggles back and forth by its own thickness. This allows you to use the same tape for inside and outside measurements.

The metal hook on the end of a tape measure is loose by its own thickness. This permits accurately taking inside and outside measurements.

A combination square helps center one piece on the other (above). The square aligns the parts, and establishes a vertical plane (right).

The speed square makes it easy to align two parts (left) and to make them square to one another (right).

DRILLS AND SCREWS

The electric drill is everyone's first power tool, and it's amazing how much drill you can buy for $30 or $40—they're genuine bargains. Reasonably good drills are so cheap and common that there is no reason to limit yourself to owning just one. For the kind of glue-and-screw construction you'll find throughout this book, it's most efficient to have two drills. Keep one tool set up for drilling pilot holes and clearance holes. Mount a screwdriver bit in the other.

Drills are sold by chuck size. The most useful general-purpose drill has a ⅜-inch chuck. A ¼-inch chuck is too small for many common attachments, while a ½-inch chuck will be mounted on a tool that's too large and too heavy for household use. The new keyless chucks are much better than the older keyed ones, plus there is no key to lose. Variable speed is

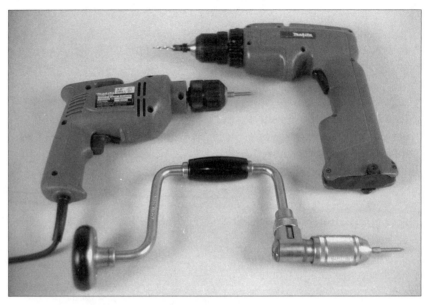

Cordless drills have rechargeable batteries in the handle (right). The corded drill has a screwdriver bit in its keyless chuck (left). An old-style brace is a low-cost alternative to electric drills.

necessary for driving screws, and so is reverse, for removing screws.

Cordless drills are more expensive, but once you've used one you won't want to go back to the copper tether. Modern rechargeable batteries pack plenty of power for woodworking projects. Ask your family to get you a ⅜-inch cordless drill for Christmas. You'll never regret it.

POOR MAN'S DRIVER

If you want more exercise from your woodworking projects, or if the luxury of having two electric drills offends you, try driving screws with an old-style bit brace. You can find a good brace at the flea market for between $5 and $10. Look for one with a free-turning ball-bearing in the knob, and make sure the chuck and its ratchet mechanism both operate. Mount a regular Phillips-head driver in the chuck. You'll find you can generate more than enough force to spin a screw down tight in no time flat. In fact you'll probably need to lighten up at the end, to avoid snapping the head off the screw. The ratchet mechanism allows you to drive and remove screws in tight spots.

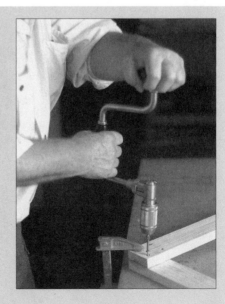

A bit brace exerts plenty of screw-driving torque.

SCREWS

There are dozens of types of wood screw at the home center. They can generally be distinguished by size, head style, driver style, and finish, as shown in the photo at right. A typical screw size is #6 × 2, where the #6 refers to the size of wire from which it was cut, and the 2 refers to its total length in inches.

The projects in this book were made with the same basic kind of outdoor construction screw that's sold by every home center in North America. They're typically #6 and #8 screws, ranging from ¾ inch to 3 inches in length, bugle-shaped head for sinking into the surface of the wood, cross-slot (Phillips) style driver, and galvanized for resistance to rust.

What size screw to use? Stick with #6 and #8 screws, and choose the longest you can fit before the point comes through the other side. The sizes we use are #6 × ¾, #6 × 1, #6 × 1 ⅝, #6 × 2, #8 × 2½, and #8 × 3. We buy them in 2-pound and 5-pound boxes. Bugle-head construction screws are endlessly useful indoors and out, and eventually you will use the whole box, so don't be seduced by expensive little packets of 10 or 12 screws.

In addition to Phillips-head screws, you may find regular single-slot screws, and square-drive Robertson screws. Slotted screws are difficult to drive with a drill. The Robertson square–

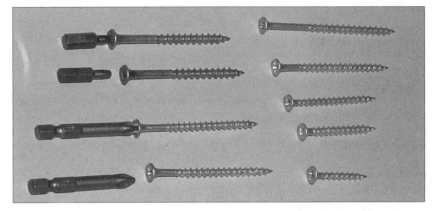

Phillips, or cross-slot, screws are easy to power-drive (bottom). Robertson, or square-drive, screws are standard in Canada and increasingly available in the States (top). The #6 screws at right range from 1 inch to 2¹/₂ inches in length.

drive style, which is standard in Canada, is an excellent alternative to the Phillips style and they are increasingly available in the U.S. market.

Pilot Holes, Clearance Holes

Clearance holes and pilot holes remove wood for screws and nails, so the wood pulls tight without splitting. A clearance hole should be the same size as or even a hair larger than the outside diameter of a screw's threads. A pilot hole can be no larger than the core diameter of a screw or nail, and ideally it should be a little smaller.

"A hair larger." "A little smaller." "No larger than." What can you do with such vague specifications? In softwood, "close" is close enough. For a #6 screw, the clearance hole should be ⁹⁄₆₄ inch, but ⅛ inch will do, and the pilot hole should be ⁵⁄₆₄ inch, but ¹⁄₁₆ will do. For a #8

screw, the clearance hole should be ¹¹⁄₆₄ inch but ³⁄₁₆ inch will do, and the pilot hole should be ⁵⁄₃₂ inch. You will never have enough drill bits to match every screw and nail, but you can make do as long as you understand what you are trying to accomplish.

Wood screws pull one piece of wood tight against the other. The pressure is exerted between the underside of the screwhead in one piece of wood, and the top face of the screw thread in the other piece of wood. This is why if you allow the screw threads to cut into the first piece of wood on their way to the second, there's no squeeze. The screw doesn't pull the way it's meant to, and the two pieces won't come tight together.

This is why it is important to drill a clearance hole through the first piece of wood. The clearance hole allows the screw threads to pass cleanly through. The clearance hole should not penetrate the second piece of

Grab a broken screw with vise-grip pliers, and twist it out of the wood.

Drill clearance holes through the first piece of wood, then drive the screws down tight. The glue squeeze-out indicates a tight joint (right).

Check the squareness of the assembly before driving the second screw.

3. Put the two pieces back together and clamp them.

4. Drill clearance holes through the top piece of wood.

5. Drive the first screw. Drive it tight enough to bury the head beneath the surface.

6. Check the alignment of the parts and if they have shifted, realign them. Then drive the remainder of the screws.

Troubleshooting

It's always possible to drive a screw so hard that the head twists off. You'll feel it let go and the head will spin freely. You will be able to tease it out of the wood with the point of a knife. When you're joining two pieces of wood face to face with a half-dozen or more screws, you can ignore the broken one. However, when you are making a joint with two or three screws in small pieces of wood, you have to remove and replace it.

Disassemble the joint before the glue sets. Remove any good screws and twist the pieces apart, exposing the broken stub. Grab it with vise-grip pliers, as shown in the photo above, and twist it out of the wood. Then scrape the semi-congealed glue off the wood and start over.

wood, though it's fine to make a pilot hole to steer the screw, and to eliminate any possibility of splitting the wood.

Combination bits for drilling clearance holes for screws typically have three different sections: A conical countersink for the screw head, a clearance section, and a pilot section. Some styles can be adjusted to suit different lengths of screw, and some can't.

Yellow glue and screws will make a permanent joint between two pieces of wood. Such a joint is stronger than the wood itself, which you can check for yourself by making a test joint and trying to break it apart. The general routine for joining wood with screws and glue has six basic steps:

1. Hold the two parts in position and draw layout lines around their intersection.

2. Take the two pieces apart so you can roll glue onto the mating surfaces, within the layout lines.

Nails with glue, and screws with glue, are interchangeable methods of joining softwood. Some people find screws easier to control, while others prefer the controlled violence of driving nails. You can substitute nails for screws, and vice versa, in most of the projects throughout this book.

For accurately made projects, the basic routine is the same for nails as for screws. It goes like this:

1. Fit the mating parts together and draw a layout line.

2. Start a couple of nails in one of the parts, then roll glue onto the mating surfaces.

3. Hold the parts together with your hand or with clamps and drive the first nail.

4. Check the alignment of the parts before you drive the second nail.

5. Drive the rest of the nails at various angles to one another, as shown in the photo at right. This dovetail effect greatly increases their holding power.

Hold the nail in position and start it into the wood with a couple of light hammer taps. Then take your holding hand out of the way and deliver four or five solid blows to drive the nail head down to the surface of the wood. Swing the hammer from your shoulder and elbow, as shown in the top photo. Aim for the surface of the wood, not for the top of the nail.

If you are new to hammers and nails, you'll probably find

Swing the hammer from your shoulder and elbow, not from your wrist. Aim for the surface of the wood, not for the head of the nail.

yourself holding the hammer handle too close to the head. This may improve your aim, but it also delivers a weak blow. Try shifting your grip back on the handle, so you can swing freely and vigorously. If you can't control the hammer when you shift your grip, try changing to a heavier hammer. Perfect your technique by driving practice nails into a scrap 2×4.

HAMMERS

There is a bewildering variety of hammers at the home center or hardware store. The choices include head weight in ounces, face shape, handle type, and claw style. The other key vari-

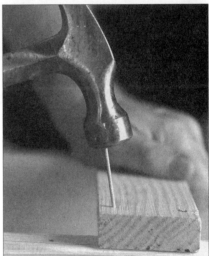

For greater holding power, drive the nails at an angle to one another, dovetail-fashion.

able is price. You don't need a professional carpenter's hammer, which can cost $100 or more, but you shouldn't make do with the cheapest hammer you can find, either. Expect to

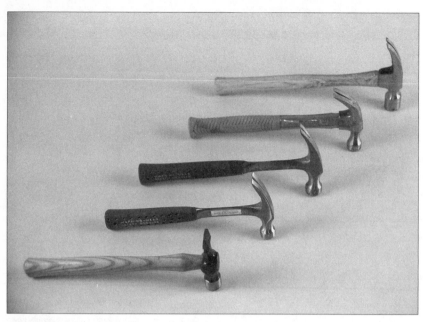

Hammers: choose the one you like. From the top: 24-ounce wooden-handled framing hammer; 16-ounce curved-claw hammer with fiberglass handle; 16-ounce framing hammer with rubber-covered steel handle; 10-ounce tack hammer; 10-ounce cross-peen cabinetmaker's hammer.

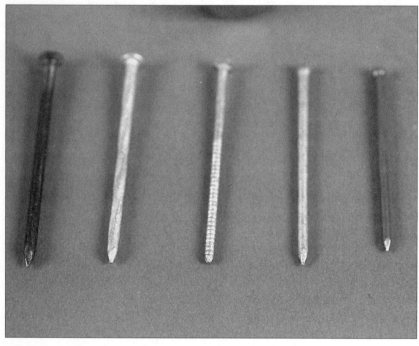

All of these are 2 ½ inch nails. From the left: common nail, galvanized spiral nail; siding or Maze nail; galvanized finishing nail; bright finishing nail.

pay between $15 and $20 for a good hammer. If you're using an old hammer, make sure the head and handle are securely mated to one another.

Weight: Most people are comfortable with a medium-weight hammer, 14 oz. or 16 oz. The weight should be stamped on the head itself. If you are new

to driving nails, consider buying two hammers, a 10-oz. lightweight, and a 16-oz. or 18-oz. heavyweight.

Face shape: The business end of the hammer is called the face. It should be almost flat, with a very small crown, and the edges should be beveled. A hammer with a pronounced crown is liable to strike a glancing blow, bending the nail.

Claw style: The choices are a curved claw or a flat claw. The flat claw works like a pry-bar and is good for rough carpentry and demolition work. The curved claw does a good job of pulling errant nails, so it's the better choice for a general-purpose hammer.

Handle: The alternatives are wood, fiberglass, or stainless steel. They're all good, so choose what feels right in your hand.

Nail-sets: Along with your hammer, buy a set of three nail-sets for driving the heads of finishing nails below the surface of the wood. The nail-set has to be at least as big as the head of the nail, which is why you need three of them.

NAILS

For outdoor projects, choose galvanized nails. They're zinc-coated so they resist rust, and their rough surface also grips the wood better than uncoated nails. In general, use regular wire nails with flat heads for construction projects, use siding nails for furniture details, and use finishing nails when you want to conceal the nailheads. For extra strength, use spiral nails, often sold as screw flooring nails.

Siding nails, or Maze nails, are especially useful for outdoor projects. These galvanized nails were designed for holding clapboard on houses. They're long and slender, with a small head and a grooved section toward the point. The point itself is blunt, which reduces the likelihood of splitting the wood. Whenever you're tempted to use a finishing nail, see whether a Maze nail would not do instead, because it will almost always do a better job.

Like a screw, the nail has to go through the first piece of wood and into the second piece. It must go at least as deep into the second piece as the thickness of the first piece. Ideally, it should go that far again, so to nail a $\frac{3}{4}$-inch piece of wood onto a 2×4, use a $2\frac{1}{2}$ inch (8d or 8-penny) nail.

When you are nailing pieces of wood together, more isn't necessarily better. When the grain of the wood runs the same way, drive nails 6 inches to 9 inches apart. When you're making a cross-grain joint, use a minimum of three nails, but never so many that the wood starts to split. As with screws, the antidote to splitting is to drill a pilot hole of about half the diameter of the nail itself.

Pulling nails

Catch the head of the nail in the claw of the hammer and lever the nail out of the wood. To protect the surface of the wood, slip

To gain leverage for pulling a nail, slip a block under the hammer head.

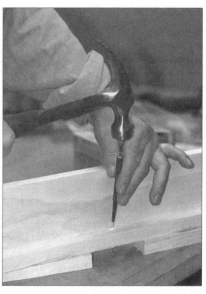

When a nail goes completely wrong, you may be able to drive it out from the back by tapping a nailset against its point.

a scrap of wood or a shingle under the hammer claw. If the nail is too high for good leverage, slip a thick block of wood under the hammer head, as shown in the photo above. If it's buried in the surface of the wood, see whether you can insert the hammer claw or a pry-bar between the pieces.

Troubleshooting

Lotsa swats: When it takes a lot of blows—more than six—to drive a nail, you aren't delivering enough energy. Extend your swing by holding the hammer farther away from its head. If you're already holding the end of the handle, switch to a heavier hammer, even if you have to choke up on its handle.

Elephant tracks: The hammer skids off the nail head and dings the wood. Check the hammer face for dirt and clean it.

Most projects can stand a few dents, but you can make one go away if you wet the dent, then steam the wood dry with a regular clothes iron.

The nail bends: Pull it out and start over with a new nail. Don't try to re-use a bent nail. If you were trying to nail into a knot, don't. You can't nail into knots.

Bad angle: If the nail is at the wrong angle, pull it out and try again. You can't change a nail's direction by pushing and pulling the portion that's still sticking out of the wood.

Bad aim: The point of the nail wanders out through the side of the wood, but you don't notice until after setting the nail head. Tap the point of the nail with the nail-set and drive it back, until you can catch the head with the hammer claw.

CAMBIUM PRESS

PO Box 909   Bethel, CT 06801
phone 203-778-2782   www.cambiumpress.com

WOODWORKER'S ESSENTIAL FACTS, FORMULAS & SHORT-CUTS
Rules of Thumb Help Figure It Out, With or Without Math

Ken Horner

Nearly every woodworking operation requires a fact, a calculation, or a reasonably close estimate. WOODWORKER'S ESSENTIAL shows how to solve woodworking problems by using math, or by following simple rules of thumb. With this fact-packed handbook on the bench, woodworkers can enjoy workshop success even if they are not comfortable making calculations.

list price, $24.95
Paperback / 312 pages / 8x10
400 black-and-white illustrations
ISBN 1-892836-15-7

APPEARANCE & REALITY:
A Visual Handbook for Artists, Designers, and Makers
Stephen Hogbin

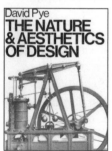

This new design handbook goes beyond tired Modernism. Hogbin examines the fundamentals of line, form, color, and pattern, then moves on to investigate such broader issues as context, gender, community, region, the enviornment, and cultural diversity - which together govern the meaning conveyed by the made object. Essential for students and important for mature designers.

list price $29.95
192 pgs, 8.5 x 10, color, paperback, ISBN 1-892836-05-X

THE NATURE AND AESTHETICS OF DESIGN
David Pye

Prof. Pye establishes a basic theory of design, in a lucid style and in jargon-free language. This book is of special importance to crafts artists, for Pye himself was an architect, industrial designer, and woodworker. He illuminates the issues confronting every thoughtful maker.

list price $22.95
160 pgs, 8.5x11, b&w, pbk,
ISBN 0-9643999-1-1

THE NATURE AND ART OF WORKMANSHIP
David Pye

In a mechanized age, does it make any sense to work with hand tools when machines can do the same job? Cutting through a century of fuzzy thinking, Prof. Pye proposes a new theory based on the concepts of "workmanship of risk", and "workmanship of certainty."

list price $22.95
160 pgs, 8.5x11, b&w, pbk,
ISBN 0-9643999-0-3

SHOP DRAWINGS FOR CRAFTSMAN INTERIORS
Cabinets, Moldings & Built-Ins
for Every Room in the Home
Measured & Drawn by Robert W. Lang

Stickley Craftsman-style homes, cottages and bungalows are among the most popular housing in America, and many books detail them in lovely color photos. This is the first and only book to present working shop drawings for carpenters and woodworkers who wish to repair or replace original Craftsman detailing, as well as for those who wish to create new work in the Craftsman style.

list price, $24.95
192 pages, 8.5 x 11, pbk
Hundreds of line drawings
ISBN 1-892836-16-5

SHOP DRAWINGS FOR CRAFTSMAN FURNITURE
27 Stickley Designs
for Every Room in the Home

list price $22.95
144 pp, 8.5 x 11, b&w, pbk.
ISBN 1-892836-12-2

MORE SHOP DRAWINGS FOR CRAFTSMAN FURNITURE
30 Stickley Designs for Every Room in the Home

list price $22.95
144 pp, 8.5 x 11, b&w, pbk.
ISBN 1-892836-14-9

Robert W. Lang

Here, at last, are accurate shop drawings of Stickley Craftsman furniture. Woodworker Bob Lang has sought authentic Craftsman antiques for measuring. Each project is complete with dimensioned orthographic views, details and sections, plus a cutting list. Projects include tables, chairs, bureaus, armoires, bookcases, desks, and plant stands. Technical introduction.

CABINETMAKING PROCEDURES
FOR THE SMALL SHOP
Kevin Fristad & John Ward

Here's an updated rundown on how commercial cabinetshops work, with advice for the ameteur as well as for the professional. Emphasizes practical standards, smart planning, accurate measurements, and organized workflow.

list price $21.95
128 pgs., 8x10, b&w, paperback,
ISBN 1-892836-11-4